Fields *of* Toil

A Migrant
Family's Journey

Toil

The Washington State University Press gratefully
acknowledges the support and assistance of the
Walla Walla Union-Bulletin and *The Seattle Times*
in the publication of this book.

Fields *of*

A Migrant Family's Journey

Toil

ISABEL VALLE

With a Foreword by Rick Doyle
of the *Walla Walla Union-Bulletin*

WSU PRESS

Washington State University Press
Pullman, Washington

Washington State University Press, Pullman, Washington 99164-5910

Library of Congress Cataloging-in-Publication Data
Valle, Isabel.
        Fields of toil : a migrant family's journey / by Isabel Valle ; foreword by Rick Doyle of the Walla Walla Union-Bulletin.
            p.   cm.
        ISBN 0-87422-101-3 (pbk. : alk. paper)
        1. Migrant labor—Texas—Social conditions—Case studies. 2. Hispanic Americans—Texas—Social conditions—Case studies. 3. Migrant agricultural laborers—Oregon—Case studies. 4. Migrant agricultural laborers—Washington (State)—Case studies. 5. Seasonal labor—Oregon—Case studies. 6. Seasonal labor—Washington (State)—Case studies.   I. Title.
HD5856.U5V35 1994
331.5'44'09764—dc20   93-33254
                                                                               CIP

Contents

Foreword

A SONG BY THE BEATLES begins with the line, "Living is easy with eyes closed, misunderstanding all you see." When it comes to migrant workers, most of us in the Northwest—and in the nation—are walking around with our eyes closed. We simply don't see them—and when we do, we apply stereotypes and prejudices to the point where we really don't understand what we see.

The best way to open people's eyes and eliminate misunderstandings is for people to get to know migrant workers and to appreciate the kind of life that they lead. At the *Walla Walla Union-Bulletin*, we decided to accept the challenge of helping people get to know a family of migrant workers and to document their lives as they moved from town to town, state to state, crop to crop.

The following is a compilation of a year-long series of newspaper articles that ran in the *Walla Walla Union-Bulletin* from July 7, 1991, to July 5, 1992, which will introduce readers to the family of Raul and Maria Elena Martinez. Isabel Valle spent a year living with, traveling with, and working in the fields with this family to help us understand the life of the migrant worker. These laborers are vital to the economy. There can be no doubt that, without these workers to harvest the crops, few fruit and vegetable farmers would be able to remain in business.

It took more than 1 1/2 years to prepare for this project. Once we decided to proceed we were faced with many dilemmas. It was immediately apparent that we would need a reporter who could speak the language. The more we pursued the project the more apparent it became that the reporter would also need to understand and appreciate the culture. The reporter would also have to be willing to devote one full year to life on the road, a life that would be physically demanding and emotionally draining.

Problem No. 1: Find a bilingual, bicultural reporter who is willing to live on the road for one year in spartan surroundings. And it would be helpful if the reporter would spend some time working in the fields under the sweltering summer sun with the migrant family.

Solution: Maria Isabel Valle. We located Isabel with the help of the National Association of Hispanic Journalists. After several telephone calls and an interview, it was clear that Isabel was the reporter for the job.

Isabel had more than six years' reporting experience. She began her career with the *Huntsville Morning News* in Texas while she was still in college. After graduation from Sam Houston University, she moved to the *Port Lavaca Wave*, a small daily newspaper in Port Lavaca, Texas. She quickly moved up to the *San Antonio Express News* where she worked for four years. She traveled extensively in Mexico reporting on politics, elections, and the Mexico City earthquake in 1985.

In January 1989, she began a one-year stint at the *Daily Journal* in Caracas, Venezuela. While at the daily English-language newspaper, she covered a variety of topics including national political riots. She was living and working under martial law during this time. She also visited Cuba for a week and reported on her visit.

After returning to the United States, Isabel decided against opportunities at several daily newspapers so she could work as a freelance writer. But what made Isabel even more qualified for this project is that her grandparents were migrant workers. Her parents, who live in San Antonio, recall life on the road when they were children. The challenge of documenting for the first time what it truly means to be a migrant worker appealed to Isabel.

Problem No. 2: Find a migrant family who would be willing to open its home and its life to a reporter. To do the best job of illustrating the life of migrants, the family should have at least one child and work in at least three states.

Solution: Knock on doors. Knock on doors. Knock on doors. Isabel spent two months networking with local Hispanics who helped her gain the confidence of the migrant population. Day after day after day, Isabel talked with families. The story was the same. One of the adult family members would say yes and the other would say no. The idea of having a reporter writing about their lives on a weekly basis for a year was more than most families were willing to consider. Until the Martinez family arrived.

Raul has spent his entire life in the fields. He knows how difficult it can be and can see the benefit of more people understanding the contribution his family and other migrant families make.

With the problems solved, we embarked on "Fields of Toil: A Migrant Family's Journey." Now, with the help of the Washington State University Press, this series has been compiled into a book. We hope it will open all of our eyes to a vital segment of our community.

Rick Doyle
Managing Editor
Walla Walla Union-Bulletin

Introduction

WHEN I WAS FIRST contacted by the *Walla Walla Union-Bulletin* in December 1990 about the idea of following a migrant family for one year, my initial reaction was: "How interesting! I too would love to know how they live – physically put myself in their shoes and get the opportunity to let others know exactly what they go through."

What I especially found intriguing was that a small newspaper in the northwest corner of the country was willing to devote one full year to publish in-depth stories about such an important issue. Most papers throughout the country may spend a few weeks or a few months on one topic, but rarely one full year. Much less, allow a reporter to dedicate herself to one story 24-hours a day for 365 days.

I began to inquire about the topic in my home state of Texas, where many migrants have a home base, and I learned that numerous people ranging from politicians to health researchers to educators were interested in learning more about the life of a migrant family. This gave me the incentive to commit myself to this project. I realized the need for it.

But I came to Washington state with a few misconceptions. I thought it was going to be easy to locate a family who would allow me into its home for one year. It wasn't. I met about 30 families and although I never had a door slammed in my face, I did find people who were wary of me. During the startup process, I learned that migrants are a proud people. They are proud of their work, they are proud of their families, and they are proud of the bond they share with other migrant families.

Many were skeptical about me. They were not too excited about having a newspaper reporter live with them and write about their private lives. So my first job was to gain their confidence. To accomplish this I sought the assistance of local Hispanic leaders. People who migrant families rely on, trust, have confidence in, and most importantly, respect. With the help of these people I was able to knock on doors and enter homes.

Although I received help from many people in many areas, there are a few I specifically need to acknowledge. Jackie Morales and Lorna Rodriguez, social workers at the Family Medical Center, allowed me to spend days with them making home-visits, which gave me the opportunity to meet and talk with some families in their surroundings. Connie Hernandez, center director of Walla Walla Migrant Headstart, helped me get an inside view of how important education is to the children of migrant parents. Hernandez and her staff have an open-door policy, not only for the parents but the public as well, and this allowed me to see the interaction between the teachers and the students.

The person who initially knocked on doors and introduced me to families at the Walla Walla Labor Camp was Arturo Martinez, with the Walla Walla Job Service Center. Martinez also gave me inside hints on how to approach migrant workers, was always thinking of innovative ways to get me introduced to the migrant community, and always let me know that he was committed to the project.

And Mary Lou Jenkins, employment coordinator at the Job Training Center. Since the first day I arrived she helped me in getting the project off the ground. Jenkins put me in contact with those I needed to meet, provided me with a lot of moral support after fruitless days of knocking on doors, and her strong belief in this project gave me the incentive to keep pushing forward. She was also the driving force in securing a one-hour radio talk show at a Hispanic radio station in Walla Walla, KSMX, which gave me the opportunity to tell the listeners a little about myself and the project. Carlos Jaques, the station's general manager, was gracious to give me the air time. These people and many more were instrumental in helping get this project rolling.

The rest was up to me. What follows is my attempt to bring readers into the home of a migrant family and to take them on the road, into the fields, and into the minds of migrant children. Through it, I hope to bring some understanding of the real life of migrant workers.

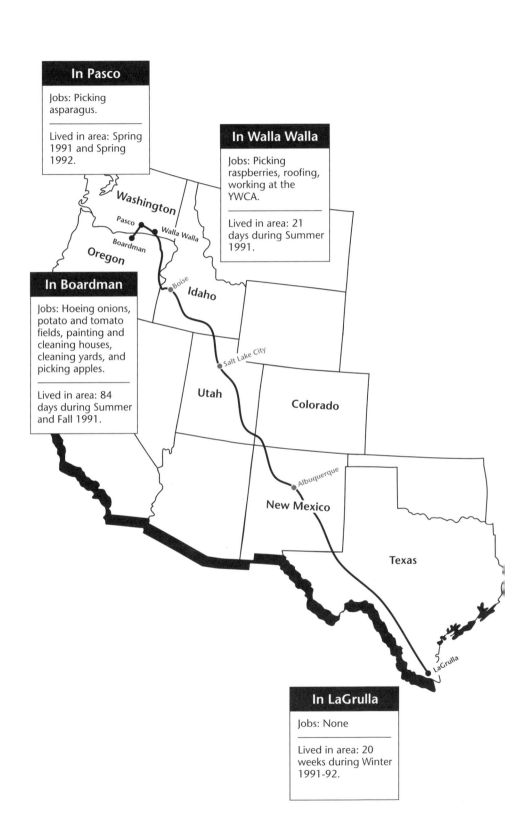

In Pasco

Jobs: Picking asparagus.

Lived in area: Spring 1991 and Spring 1992.

In Walla Walla

Jobs: Picking raspberries, roofing, working at the YWCA.

Lived in area: 21 days during Summer 1991.

In Boardman

Jobs: Hoeing onions, potato and tomato fields, painting and cleaning houses, cleaning yards, and picking apples.

Lived in area: 84 days during Summer and Fall 1991.

In LaGrulla

Jobs: None

Lived in area: 20 weeks during Winter 1991-92.

Washington

Pasco

Walla Walla

Boardman

Oregon

Boise

Idaho

Salt Lake City

Utah

Colorado

Albuquerque

New Mexico

Texas

LaGrulla

Chapter 1

The Migrant Life

WHEN WORK IS SCARCE, but the need for money is pressing, often there is no other choice for migrant workers but to travel about the country seeking employment. The constant relocating, never staying in one place long enough to establish roots, and the hard, manual labor that they face just to earn a minimum wage, is nearly unbearable. But this lifestyle has been followed for many years by many people.

When speaking to migrants about their lives they are quick to point out that many of their number have died working in the fields or while traveling. To some people this may sound unbelievable, but for migrant workers it is simply a way of life. For the past 35 years, Raul and Maria Elena Martinez have left their home in LaGrulla, Texas, located at the southern tip of Texas about three miles north of the Rio Grande River (the "South Texas Valley") in search of a better life. But in many instances, their expectations have been shattered.

"This isn't an easy life. We've had to live in the worst conditions. Looking and finding work is never easy and when you have children, babies, that just makes this life much harder," Maria Elena, 52, recalls.

During the years following their marriage in 1956, the Martinezes limited their search for work to Texas, where they picked cotton, oranges, and a variety of vegetables. But with droves of other families following their footsteps, the Martinezes realized that their only hope of finding more jobs and earning a little more money was to leave the state. Through communication with other migrant families they heard of work and headed to California, Illinois, Michigan, Minnesota, and Washington to try to make a living.

The hard part, they say, is never knowing what they are going to encounter along the road or at their destination. Slipping from Spanish into English, often struggling to find the right words in English, the Martinezes recall arriving in labor camps to find they have to live in chicken coops equipped with one outdoor toilet for 20 people. In other cases, milk was scarce so coffee was substituted in the baby bottles.

"During this time I had children so we were traveling with babies," says Maria Elena.

In early spring each year, Raul and Maria Elena load their pickup truck with personal belongings. One by one, the younger of their 13 children pile into the vehicle, ready to leave Texas and travel the country in search of work with their parents. As with most migrant families, some years their destinations are mapped out in advance, but other years they have no clue as to where they may be going.

"Move to where we can find some work," Raul keeps repeating in Spanish. "If we don't find any there, then we'll move somewhere else."

This year, they came to Washington state to pick asparagus, one of the hardest kinds of work they say there is. Raul, 61, and Maria Elena traveled with their sons Charlie, 15, Jimmy, 10, and Billy, 7; their daughter, Doris, 20; and son Danny, 28, his wife Alicia, 26, and their two children. They arrived in Pasco, Washington, in March and picked in the fields until the last days of June. Halfway through the harvest, the work took its toll on Doris and she returned to LaGrulla.

"I felt so sorry for her. She would finish full bottles of Tylenol for her backaches and after a while [the pills] stopped taking effect," her mother recalls. Doris, a first-year student at Texas State Technical Institute, decided to work in the fields so she could earn enough money to purchase a car. She had been offered a job at a hospital in Texas, and a car was a necessity.

"But she just couldn't make it. It's hard work and they're out there killing themselves," says Maria Elena. "It's too hard to be bending over all day long. I would see many women that would stop work and cry in the middle of the fields. Doris was one of them."

Once the asparagus harvest was over, the Martinezes arrived in Walla Walla in July with hopes of working the sweet onion harvest. It is here that I join their household. Meanwhile, Danny and his family have decided to return to Texas after they too found that the work in the fields was physically demanding with very low pay. On their way home, their truck overturned near Tremonton, Utah, when Danny fell asleep behind the wheel. Fortunately, no one was seriously injured. Family members suffered only minor cuts and bruises.

Upon their arrival in Walla Walla, the Martinezes have found that jobs in harvesting sweet onions are scarce. Raul spent every night of the first week calling and visiting farmers in hopes of getting hired. The answers were always the same: "There's no work now, call back tomorrow and maybe we'll have something." Raul paces the house wondering how he is going to earn some money. Every day that migrants do not work is a day of lost wages that are so desperately needed.

"We need to work every day because if we don't we lose a lot of money. We may not earn money every day but we do spend it every day," Raul says. There's food to be bought to feed a family of five — which includes three growing boys — gas to fill the truck, and toiletries and other necessary items.

"All of this takes money. Things are expensive and when you have only about $600, you start to panic," Maria Elena adds.

Walla Walla, Washington: Mid-Summer

Since work in the onion fields seems long in coming, Raul has decided to look for other employment. In the two weeks they have been in Walla Walla, Raul and the family have earned money doing yard work and other odd jobs in order to make ends meet. The younger children are also looking for jobs and can be found working beside their father.

"That's what we have to do when jobs in the fields are not found, we have to find work anywhere, doing anything," Maria Elena says.

Once Raul finds work, a sense of relief takes over and the expression on his face changes. Although the work he does is hard manual labor, at night he walks around the house with a great sense of accomplishment.

"I'm happy when I'm working," Raul says with a shy smile. "I like to work and I like all kinds of work." On the days that he has no luck finding employment, Raul picks up litter around the house, washes his truck, cleans inside the house, or just walks around looking for things to fix. Raul's latest work is roofing, a job he obtained through an acquaintance.

"That's the way he is, he can never just sit around, he always has to be busy," Maria Elena says. "But what really makes him happy is that he's earning some money. Right now we only have enough to buy food. We still need money for the road, and we'd like to have a little saved up for the winter, when there is no work."

Work is a major priority for the rest of the family as well. The children have found themselves bored staying at home. The two younger children pass their days bouncing a basketball around the house or playing with neighborhood children. Charlie spends his days listening to music or looking after his younger brothers. Maria Elena keeps herself very busy cooking, cleaning, washing, and looking after the house.

But once they talk about working and earning money, their spirits brighten. Maria Elena and the children have found a job picking raspberries in nearby Milton-Freewater, Oregon. Although the idea of having to start the day at 4 a.m. may not be too appealing to the children, once they are physically dragged out of bed, placed in the car, and driven to the field, they wake up and start talking about what they are going to do with the money they earn. Charlie, meanwhile, has found employment through the Walla Walla Job Training Center. He will be working at the YWCA three times a week. The days that he is not scheduled to work, he will go to the fields with the other members of the family to pick berries. The money he earns will be spent on clothes for high school this fall.

"All my family are hard workers," Raul says. "I want them to work so they can learn about making a living."

"I want them to work in the fields so they can see how hard it is and that way they will see the importance of a good education," Maria Elena emphasizes.

Raul adds, "We stress education to our children because it's very important and no matter what state we are in, we will always send the children back to Texas to continue school, or we will enroll them in a local school."

Although the oldest children have completed their high school education and some have even gone on to get some form of technical training, their income still comes from working in the fields. "That's because there are no jobs in the [South Texas] valley. There is nothing for us there, so every year it's the same thing, travel the country looking for work," Raul says.

"I don't want my children to come looking for work anymore. I want them to have a good job in the [South Texas] valley and a good paying job, at least $6 an hour, because they have suffered enough," Maria Elena stresses. "I've lived this way all my life and I don't want the same thing for my kids."

The Martinezes hope that factories will someday employ local residents in South Texas. "If [industries] can open up factories in Mexico and other Latin American countries so they can get cheap labor, why can't they do the exact thing in the valley? We may not be able to earn a lot of money, but at least we can stay in our homes," Maria Elena says.

With the burden of traveling from place to place in search of work comes the additional frustration of packing belongings into large green garbage bags, loading trucks to full capacity where not even the smallest space is left empty, looking for affordable housing where there is at least running water and sanitary conditions, and finally, finding food to feed the family. But even with all these deplorable conditions, the Martinezes say the worst thing they must endure is looking for work.

"The hardest part of migrant living is that when your work ends there is nothing else and you're left desperately seeking some way to get money to support your family," Raul says. "That has got to be the worst feeling, not knowing where your next paycheck will come from."

The future doesn't look bright for the Martinez family for the rest of the year. Crops throughout the country have dwindled due to severe drought or freezing temperatures, and yet with every passing day an influx of migrant workers keeps traveling down the roads looking for work. At the same time, Raul would like to retire soon and Maria Elena would love to someday settle permanently in their Texas home. The children too would like to remain in Texas where they can continue going to school with their friends. But for now the days are filled with discussions of where they have heard there is a good harvest and good pay, and how long it will take to travel to such locations.

"I think we're going to continue this way of life until we get a good job somewhere in Texas," Maria Elena says.

"Or anywhere," Raul answers.

A Rude Awakening

The "way of life" which Maria Elena has described to me is anything but comfortable. Although some of my distant relatives worked in the fields many years ago, the only thing I knew about fruits and vegetables was what I saw displayed at the grocery store. Working in the fields with the Martinez family has been a rude awakening.

To begin with, I'm not a morning person, so having to suddenly start my days at 4 a.m. did not come easy. Maria Elena and I were the first to wake up when the alarm went off. The kitchen was the first place she headed, to brew fresh coffee and prepare flour tortillas, scrambled eggs, and refried beans. We made tacos and wrapped them in foil to eat later during a break from the field work. We quickly put on our working clothes, which consist of a pair of old blue jeans, old tennis shoes, a cotton T-shirt, a long-sleeve shirt to go over it, and a hat.

The next, and probably most difficult task, was waking up the children. Calling out their names to arouse them did no good. Neither did shaking them a bit. We found that the only thing that worked was dragging 10-year-old Jimmy from under the covers and into the bathroom to wash his face and get him dressed. With Billy, 7, we had a harder time. Maria Elena had to kneel beside him and dress him while he was still sound asleep on the floor.

By this time it was usually 4:45 a.m., and we had to be in the fields at 5 o'clock. So we quickly piled into the car and took our 10-minute drive into Milton-Freewater to the raspberry field. During the short drive, the cool morning breeze and the music blaring from the radio woke everyone up and the children started talking about how they would spend the money they hoped to earn that day. One of the things that impressed me most about the Martinez family is how at an early age the children learn the importance of work. They know that without working, there is no money.

Once we arrived in the fields, everyone immediately went to work, since they knew what to do — except me. I had to keep asking them questions, observing what they did while I followed in their footsteps. Picking raspberries is not hard physical labor, but it is tedious. The children and Maria Elena moved through the raspberry fields, fighting their way through weeded rows. With their hands and arms they moved the slightly thorned vines out of the way to get to the raspberries. Within just a few minutes, I found that my arms and hands were scratched from the thorns. The children laughed at me because I was constantly yelling, "Ouch!" Our hands were also covered with the red juice of the berries.

After about an hour, the children started getting tired, especially Billy. So instead of picking berries, we put him to work as an errand boy getting us water and more empty flats. Later, the boys decided that all they wanted to do was play. In two instances, the boys were running up and down the rows and stumbled on one of the flats we had filled, spilling all of the raspberries onto the ground. I couldn't help but laugh. Maria Elena became furious, and I later learned why.

In the five hours we worked, we filled 14 flats. Two days later when we went to pick up our pay we found we earned $23. At that moment, I remembered the two flats the boys stumbled over. I realized how precious every picked raspberry is in order to earn money to support a family. The children thought $23 was a sufficient amount. Maria Elena didn't say anything.

I thought, "How can farm workers survive like this? They work such long hours to barely earn a penny?" Putting it in terms I'm familiar with, I divided the amount earned into the hours worked to find that it came to about $4.60 an hour. However, there were four of us working, so it really added up to only $1.15 an hour. This is how some migrant families live year after year.

After thinking about it for a while, Maria Elena has decided she no longer wants to pick berries. "It's not worth the time for the small amount that is earned," she exclaims.

The children, however, keep insisting that once their father finished his temporary jobs and joined us in the fields, the money earned would increase. Charlie, too, said he wanted to continue working in the fields on the days he was not scheduled to work at his temporary job at the YWCA.

"Even if we make only $5, that's better than sitting at home not earning anything," he tells his mother. I learned that Charlie, at age 15, already has the worker's mentality of his father—it's a necessity to do any type of work because money is needed. Charlie goes to sleep repeatedly asking his mother, "Are we going to go pick berries in the morning?" The younger children go to sleep begging their mother not to take them to the field in the morning.

With everyone asleep on the floor, on mattresses or on the sofa in our four-room rental home, I lay awake on my mattress thinking about the flats that were stumbled over.

Then and Now: A U.S. Congressman's Reminiscences of the Migrant Life

Low pay. Long hours. Oppressive heat. Lack of jobs. Lack of housing. Lack of medical care. Lack of education.

These are the things migrant workers had to deal with 50 years ago. But that was then. This is now.

Low pay. Long hours. Oppressive heat. Lack of jobs...

People who were migrant workers nearly a half-century ago recall the days when there was no housing, no provisions for medical assistance, and no indoor plumbing. Nearby rivers were used for drinking water. And only on weekends did they go into "el pueblo" to buy groceries. One person who remembers spending his childhood days on the road is Albert Bustamante, a U.S. representative. Bustamante was elected to represent Texas' 23rd Congressional District, which includes more than 200 miles of the Rio Grande River Valley.

"I remember we used to go to Walla Walla and work there every year and now some of my family has settled in the northwest part of the country. I have family in Woodburn, Oregon," the congressman says during an interview in his San Antonio office. Like all typical migrant families, the Bustamantes would leave home in Asherton, Texas, located about 70 miles southwest of San Antonio, to travel the country looking for work in the fields.

"I remember we lived in quarters that were only two rooms, one was the kitchen and the other was the bedroom. We were 11 children, and I remember I would sleep in the kitchen because the bedroom was too crowded and it was hard to breath."

One of the worst problems they had to face, the congressman says, was the lack of medical treatment. "There was probably little to no access to health clinics. We were always getting sick because of the chemicals used on the crops, plus all the regular childhood illnesses, and we had nowhere to go."

Even with the difficulties he faced and the hard life his family lived, Bustamante notes that since they knew no other way of life, they did not realize the hardships they were going through. "There was nothing to compare our life to and everyone we knew lived like we did so it didn't matter. As long as we had a place to sleep and food to eat, we were happy."

Things have changed some since then. Today, in some labor camps, housing has improved. For example, before the Walla Walla Farm Labor Camp was established in 1940, it was fairly common to see migrant families living in tents along the roadside. Today there are 128 one-bedroom to four-bedroom apartments and four trailer spaces in the camp.

Health care assistance has also been made available. In the late 1960s, day care centers opened, and in more recent years state and federal dollars have been allocated to fund educational programs designed to give children a "head start" on education before they start school. And a major improvement for today's farm workers is the installation of portable toilets in the fields. In some areas of the country, states have established a network to keep track of children as they move from state to state. This networking is used for educational purposes, and Washington, Oregon, Idaho, California, and Texas work together to provide some assistance to migrant families.

"Congress has been looking into housing, health, water, nutrition, and environmental problems in order to improve conditions, but I feel there is still a lot more we need to study," Bustamante says. "One very good program is the Headstart program because it is a great educational tool, and they provide well balanced nutrition. Sometimes, that's the only good meal these children will eat."

But even with the improvements that have been made, migrant workers say there is still a long way to go. Sitting in his comfortable office, sipping coffee, and reflecting on his childhood, Bustamante takes a deep breath and says, "it's a terrible cycle to be in." Is there a way to break the cycle? For migrant children especially, there are opportunities.

Walla Walla Job Training Center

The only type of work that 15-year-old Charlie Martinez has known since he was a small boy is working in the fields alongside his family. His work experience includes picking fruits and vegetables, and doing other forms of manual labor. But this summer, Charlie has found new employment. He is working as a recreational aide with the Walla Walla YWCA's summer Fun Factory. He serves as a leader in this capacity, having children ages 5 through 12 who look to him for guidance and support. After a full day's work, he arrives home looking tired, but always with a smile on his face. When asked how he enjoys his job Charlie responds, "I like it, I think it's fun."

This job, obtained through the Walla Walla Job Training Center, allows Charlie to earn a few dollars to buy his clothes for high school this fall. But most importantly, it provides self-esteem and teaches him that there are other things besides field work that he is capable of doing.

The Job Training Center is a federally funded agency that places teenagers, young adults, and even older adults into jobs in the public and private sectors. The center offers assistance to economically disadvantaged people as well as those who are physically and mentally handicapped. Charlie and about 70 other youths from throughout Walla Walla work under the Summer Youth Employment program, which is geared to young people ages 14 through 21. To be eligible for the program, Charlie's family income had to be below the lower, living-standard income guidelines as established by the Department of Labor; he had to be a resident of Walla Walla County; and he had to be eligible to work in the United States. Charlie met all these requirements.

"The purpose of the Summer Youth Employment program is to give young people an appreciation for the world of work, to introduce them to the demands of work, supervisors, and co-workers," explains Steve Moss, the center's project director. For many of the students, this is their first job outside of the home. They learn what employers expect from them and, most importantly, they learn responsibility, Moss says. Charlie is eligible for the program because of his economic situation. But to meet the center's guidelines, he must remain in contact with the center after his family has left the area and inform it about his schooling and other jobs he has obtained.

There are other programs offered at the center as well, including Work Experience, where youths can work a maximum of 35 hours a week in a non-profit organization to gain employment experience and develop good work habits. Some of the jobs include working in maintenance, janitoring, recreation, and food service, and as secretarial and clerical helpers. Throughout Walla Walla, children of former migrant workers who have settled in the area during the past few years have taken advantage of the programs. Two such people are Jorge Rodriguez, 14, and Lisa Arias, 17.

Jorge works as a janitor assistant at Garrison Middle School. He comes from a family of seven, and his parents are seasonal labor workers. Lisa, who comes from a family of six, is currently a secretary assistant at Walla Walla High School. Her parents are also seasonal workers.

"I've worked in a grocery store and I've also picked grapes. During school last year, I worked as a tutor for students at Blue Ridge Elementary, but I think I like this job the best," Lisa says. Lisa's family has been traveling to and from Arizona, her home state, for the past two years. "Every six months we move but I hope this time we stay here for good."

Another program offered by the Job Training Center is the Try-Out Youth Employment, in which youths are placed in private, for-profit businesses to gain experience working in the "real world." Jaime Garcia, 17, works under this program at Pizza Hut in the Blue Mountain Mall. Jaime is from a family of 11, and the only work his parents know is harvesting fruit.

"I consider this my first job because the only other thing I've done is field work picking apples and cherries, and that's not much of a reference. Now when I go apply for something else, I will write down that

I have worked in Pizza Hut and I will have good references." At work, Jaime is responsible for making pizzas, washing dishes, and doing a variety of other chores. "I like making pizzas the most," he says. Originally from California, Jaime and his family have been in Walla Walla for the past four years.

Moss said he receives great joy in seeing some of his former trainees now successfully holding jobs in the local community. "I see them now and they're in their mid- to late-20s and they tell me that we were their first job." Teenagers are not the only ones who are helped by the Job Training Center. "Adults are also eligible for some of our programs, which include working directly with an employer. We also work very closely with the community college to try to provide them with some vocational skills or help them get their high school diplomas."

Through these and numerous other programs, migrant families who move into another part of the country have discovered that they can find employment other than in the fields, and can give something back to the community.

Fall Harvest: No jobs

Through the summer, unusual weather plagues the Walla Walla area and other parts of the country, causing severe damage. Crops freeze or are washed away. Farmers throughout Walla Walla note that June's heavy rains are causing portions of the sweet onion crop to rot, some reporting that up to 25 percent of the crop is damaged. So, fewer farm workers are needed. In some cases, farmers hire crews, but then don't have enough work for them. The word circulating among the migrant community is that work in the fields is hard to find not only in Walla Walla but anywhere in the country.

"Some of the migrant families that we met in Pasco went up to the Seattle coast when the asparagus finished last month and now they are heading back to Texas because they couldn't find any work," Maria Elena says. These families were expecting to pick blueberries and raspberries, but found coastal crops damaged by cold weather.

"It costs more money traveling looking for work than it would returning to Texas. You spend money on gas and food, and if you're going to spend the night somewhere then you try to cram everyone into a $20 a night hotel. After all this, you hopefully try to save a little of the money you earned working in the fields. That's why sometimes it's better to go home with the little money you make than try to travel around looking for more work."

Maria Elena says it costs about $300 in gas, plus food and lodging, to get from Washington to Texas. "Right now that is my biggest worry, that we won't have enough money for the road, much less for the winter when we don't work."

The murmur among the migrant families is that work can still be found in Minnesota and as far away as Florida, but will families take the risk of traveling that far and finding a situation similar to the one here?

"I don't know?" Maria Elena says sounding wary. "I have no idea what my husband has planned." As it turned out, the Martinezes didn't have to go that far.

The Search for Work: To Boardman, Oregon

After three unsuccessful weeks of looking for steady work in the Walla Walla area, Raul and Maria Elena and their three boys have packed all their belongings into their truck and moved about 90 miles southwest to Boardman, Oregon. Raul could not support his family on the few temporary jobs he was getting in Walla Walla, and the fact that some days found him without work left him feeling desperate.

"We don't like to have little jobs here and there, we like to have something where we know we will be working for at least a few weeks to a month," Raul says in Spanish.

"For example, before we went to Walla Walla we were in Pasco, picking asparagus, and that was from April to June and we liked that," Maria Elena explains. "But working every now and then and then having some days when we don't have work at all is something we're not used to."

Last year, the Martinezes worked the potato harvest in Boardman, and that is what they hope to do this year. So far, Raul has earned about $300 working at odd jobs while in Walla Walla and about $4,000 cutting asparagus in Pasco. Charlie was earning about $100 a week in his summer job at the YWCA, and he still had about a month left of work. The money he was earning would have helped him buy his school clothes this fall, but his father still felt that it was best for the family to leave Walla Walla and look for work elsewhere.

"My husband is the one that supports the family and even though Charlie was earning good money at a fun job, we had to leave so Raul could find a job," Maria Elena says. "Beside, Charlie can find a job working anywhere with his father."

Raul and Maria Elena's eldest son, Raul Martinez Jr., 34, his wife Iris, and their 4-year-old daughter Abby, are also in Boardman where Raul Jr. is working at Columbia Livestock, a local farm owned by Bob Muller. Like his father, Raul Jr. migrates from LaGrulla to the northwest part of the country every year in search of work. Raul Sr. hopes to get a job working with his son: "I worked [at that farm] last year and they know me and they know that I am a hard worker so I think I will be hired again this year."

"We hope he gets a job here or else we have to see where else we go," Maria Elena says.

With the move, the family has to resettle in a new rental apartment, in a new community, in a new state. But even if the location is new, there are many circumstances that remain the same. There is the task of having to pack and unpack a truck, stock up on food, go to the local welfare department to sign up for food stamps, and visit the food bank to see what food they can get.

The task of looking for housing was not difficult. The family immediately found a vacancy in an apartment complex where they had stayed before. The welfare department will defray the $275 (plus utilities) monthly rent, and the Martinezes are not required to put down a deposit. The apartment is unfurnished, so Raul and Maria Elena contact friends of relatives to see if anyone has some furniture that can be spared.

As Maria Elena spends the evening of their first day in their new home unpacking and putting things away in kitchen cupboards, she gives a deep sigh and repeats a common theme, "How horrible it is to always have to keep moving. It really tires you out, but that's the only way we can live."

Three Rules for Life on the Road

Never make plans. Always be ready to move. Adjust.

If there is anything I am learning about migrant living, it is the three rules above. It amazes me how families can decide overnight to move out of their current residence and into a new community, and how they immediately pack all their belongings, load their trucks, and are ready to hit the road early the next morning.

When the Martinez family moved from Pasco to Walla Walla on July 1, what struck me the most was that within four hours, they had cleared out of their trailer in Pasco, moved to Walla Walla, unpacked, and "set up house" in a rental apartment in the south side of the city. Now, at the end of July, they did the exact same thing during their move to Boardman. It took me one full night and an entire morning just to pack my bedroom.

Another important aspect I've learned from the Martinezes is "don't establish ties with anyone or anything." I learned we were moving to Boardman one day in advance. This meant having to pack immediately. Aside from that, I still had an apartment lease to attend to, utilities to take care of, banking to do, forwarding addresses to leave, plans to cancel, and farewells to say.

The Martinezes packed and left.

This is how they are used to living. They purposely try to find housing in labor camps where rent is paid on a weekly or monthly basis. Rule No. 1: long-range plans are not made.

When they are setting up house, they unpack only the necessities. Clothes usually remain stored in large green trash bags, and are unpacked as needed. Rule No. 2: always be ready to move.

What I also find amazing is how they quickly find comfort in strange and unfamiliar surroundings. The Martinezes had no trouble in setting up house in Walla Walla or now in Boardman. Upon arrival, the two younger boys, Billy and Jimmy, roamed the neighborhood in search of new friends or old ones. Charlie, like his father, will walk about the apartment inspecting things and checking out what needs to be fixed, if anything. And Maria Elena will head to the kitchen to familiarize herself with the stove, oven, and other appliances.

Their first night is passed with sound, restful sleep. I'm usually tossing and turning. This is where Rule No. 3 comes in: adjust.

With the amount of time migrant families spend on the road, it's no wonder that they live by these three rules. However, when they have settled in to field work for awhile, other guidelines are observed.

"It's Good to Be a Hard Worker"

When members of the Martinez family speak of "el patron," or the boss, they usually speak highly of him. Raul, who has been working in the fields since he was a young boy, says that a good "patron" is someone who will let his employees bring home some of the food that has been harvested.

"Some of the 'patrones' will leave boxes and boxes of the fruit or vegetable out in the fields so that the poor people can come and get what they need for free," he says. "Those are the ones we like be-cause it shows us that they are willing to give what they have to others who don't have much."

In each field that Raul has been working, he has been able to gather some of the crop and bring it home with him each evening. In the past few months, the apartment has been filled with burlap sacks of pota-toes, tomatoes, onions, and now apples. And since there is such an abundance of vegetables and fruits, the Martinezes share what they have with relatives and neighbors.

Another important aspect of a good boss is his understanding in cases where workers are ill. The Martinezes have not had any prob-lems in this regard either.

"Well, Raul won't go to the doctor if he gets sick, but that's be-cause he doesn't want to miss one day's work. It has nothing to do with the boss," says Maria Elena. "But in the times that I've gotten sick and not showed up to work, the boss will always tell my husband, 'That's a good reason.'"

The Martinezes say they have always had a good rapport with their employers and have never complained of lack of water or other facili-ties. And every year they are called back to work with the same farmers.

"These people know I am a good, hard worker and they all want me back. I don't believe in being lazy," says Raul. "There are some people who will try to goof off when they work, but that doesn't get them anywhere because all that happens is they end up getting fired."

When working in the fields, Raul is usually the first one out hoe-ing or picking. He never misses a day. He usually stays until the sun is about to set, and sometimes he is known to skip his lunch break because he doesn't want to miss a minute's work. He attributes the fact that he has proven himself as the reason he is always called back or referred from one farmer to another.

He believes that people must work hard in order to be treated right, and that is something he has instilled in his children. When Charlie was working the fields with him, Charlie could sometimes be heard complaining about the job. His father would always turn around and say in Spanish, "Be quiet, Charlie, and start working. Don't be lazy! It's good to be a hard worker. And if 'el patron' sees that you do good work, then they will always call you back." Raul's work ethic has given him an advantage over hundreds of migrant workers who compete seasonally for jobs.

Those Left in Line

Prior to the start of harvest, migrant workers – both men and women, young and old – rush to the personnel office to submit applications for employment. This year, word spreads quickly throughout the migrant community that workers are needed to harvest potatoes, onions, apples, and other crops. As early as 6 a.m., lines begin to form as people crowd around the locked entrance doors. Those waiting in line are full of questions. "I wonder how many workers they'll need this year?" "I wonder how long the harvest will last?" "I wonder how much they pay?" "I wonder if I'll get hired?"

A few hours later, movement can be seen indoors and excitement builds outside. But by this time the number of people waiting to apply has grown from about 20 to a couple of hundred. The doors open and people enter shoving and pushing, racing to sign their names on a sheet of paper with the rest of the applicants. They know that the lower their names appear on the list, the less chance they have for getting hired.

For the past few weeks, I've placed myself among the migrant workers seeking employment. I go with Maria Elena and some of her friends and relatives, and am careful not to say a word. Maria Elena speaks for all of us, and when I do talk, it's only in Spanish. In some cases, I've had to fill out applications that ask for past field work experience. I fill in the blanks with the word "none." Maria Elena says I have to come up with a believable explanation as to why I haven't worked before. We create the following scenario: I was married, but my husband left me and I now have to support myself and my three children. I never had to use that explanation, however, because I was never hired.

This application process taught me two things: migrant workers are most likely to be rehired by employers for whom they worked before, or where they are recommended by someone whose opinion is respected. Luckily, the Martinez family has had little difficulty in finding work. They have excellent recommendations and are always called back.

"We're hard workers, and everyone knows that. They know we like to work and that I don't believe in being lazy," Raul says in Spanish.

Three weeks ago, Raul and Maria Elena were called to work to pick apples for Western Empires Corporation, located about seven miles east of Boardman. They were recommended for the job by the landlord of their apartment complex. Maria Elena was unable to go because of medical problems, but Raul has gone to the fields every day from 7 a.m. to about 5 p.m. Raul has never picked apples before, but says he likes it. However, every night his wife rubs his shoulders and back to help ease the pain. He has fallen off the ladder three times in the orchard.

"Pay is good," Raul says. "We get $7 for each box we fill." He normally fills eight boxes a day, but sometimes it's 10 and other days only six. The money will be used to get the family back to Texas this fall.

Every afternoon, Raul will come home with sacks filled with apples he has picked. "The patron is real nice. He lets us bring home some of the fruit," Raul says. Lately, the apartment has been filled with the aroma of freshly baked apple pies. The family shares what it has with other family members and friends. Although the Martinez family hasn't suffered from lack of work, hundreds of others have. When I was notified that I would not be hired, I shrugged it off.

"I really don't need this job," I thought. "I'm just doing it to see what it's like." But I looked around me and saw many others who also were not hired. Their faces were filled with despair. Men and women carrying babies in their arms walked slowly to their cars after they were told there would be no room for them in the harvest. Words aren't spoken but their eyes ask, "Now what?" As one couple was getting into their car, the woman told her husband, "Don't worry. You still have applications in at two other farms. One of those will hire you."

Near one car, a group of about five men were huddled around, each one of them shaking his head and complaining in Spanish, "If they know they are only going to need 65 people in their crew, then why do they sign up over 200 people? All that is doing is giving the rest of us false hope." Another man said, "They should say right from the beginning that they are going to hire those that worked last year."

Shortly, another man approaches and tells them that applications are going to be taken the next day to work the potato harvest. With a deep sigh, one man says, "Well then, we'll go tomorrow and see what they tell us there."

Chapter 2

Housing: From Chicken Coops to Trailers

"CHICKEN COOPS. We used to live in houses that looked like chicken coops," Maria Elena says with a serious look on her face.

She recalls three years before when she, her husband, and their five youngest children lived in a one-room house while they worked the fields in Michigan. "I remember when we first got there I looked around and I said, 'Look at all those chicken coops!' Then the farmer told us that was where we were living," she recalls, laughing. "It was dirty. There were a few portable toilets for quite a lot of people and they were always filled to the top. I knew I was going to get sick."

Maria Elena also recalls that showers were taken outdoors. There was a wooden fence that surrounded the camp; a curtain made out of sheets was then hung in one corner of the fence and that is where they stood to take their showers. "We had to carry the water in buckets from inside the house," she says.

The only furniture in the one-room house was a tiny stove and table. The family slept on bunk beds, although at times some of them left the crowded quarters to sleep in the car. After a month of living in these conditions, they secured housing in another location with the help of one of Maria Elena's brothers. "He came to visit us, and he couldn't believe we were living there," she says. "Oh I just can't stand thinking about those days!"

Maria Elena also recalls her childhood when she, as one of a family of eight, traveled the country. "In one place in Texas where we worked, we all slept in the back of a truck that was used for transporting cotton. We used to sleep on top of the cotton and hang a net canopy over it to keep the mosquitoes away." In another state, she recalls having to live in a storage shed that was shared with other families. The shed was completely empty, and the only privacy the families had was the sheets that hung from the ceiling to divide their "living quarters."

Within the past couple of years, however, living conditions have improved dramatically for Maria Elena and her family. In Pasco, from

April through June, the family lived in a labor camp consisting of two- and three-bedroom trailers. The grounds and the trailers were well kept. The labor camp was rent-free during the residents' employment, with housing costs funded by farmers.

On moving to Walla Walla, the Martinezes rented a three-room apartment with a kitchen and bathroom in the city's south end. Rent was $300 a month plus utilities. When the Martinezes moved to Boardman on July 22, they found even better quality housing: a two-bedroom apartment with air conditioner and dishwasher, and a swimming pool for the apartments' tenants. The family receives a housing subsidy from the state to defray the $270 (plus utilities) rent. Here in Boardman, the only thing the family lacks is furniture. There is only a table and two picnic benches in the apartment. "This is really a nice place and so clean. We really like it here," Maria Elena says.

She notes that her family was able to find better housing because they have lived in Boardman in the past; therefore, the landlord is familiar with them. And their eldest son and his family also live in the same complex, as they have for the past few years. "Plus I help out by cleaning the pool and laundry room, and Raul will mow all the lawn."

The apartment complex was set up a few years ago to house migrants. Since the Martinezes are well-known and respected throughout Boardman and in the migrant community, other families who have difficulty in finding housing often come to the Martinezes seeking help. When this happens, Maria Elena will go talk to the managers of the surrounding apartments to see if there is any space available and to put in a good word for the newly arrived family. In many instances she has been able to secure housing for those who come knocking at the door.

"I feel so bad for people who are suffering and don't have a place to stay, especially if they have children. God has been so good to us that I feel we have to share some of that with others." The Martinezes acknowledge their good fortune in securing comfortable and affordable housing, for in Boardman and other communities such accommodations are scarce.

Migrant Housing in Boardman

Boardman, Oregon, founded in 1904 by Samuel Herbert Boardman, of Salem, is a small agricultural community of almost 1,500 citizens. Its chief employer is LambWestern, a local plant that manufactures french fries and other potato products. Two other large employers are Oregon Potato, a dehydrated potato and potato flake plant, and Big River Farm, which packages and sends potatoes to big markets. Numerous vegetable and fruit farms also surround the community, one being an onion field in which Raul and Charlie find work when they first arrive.

According to Gene Allen, the city manager, about 25 percent of the population are Hispanics who have settled in the area. "We have quite a bit of Hispanics that have assimilated in the community. And most of these people are year-round workers because the plants are open about 11 months out of the year." In the community there is a primary school—Boardman Elementary—for kindergarten to sixth grade; seventh and eighth graders are bused to nearby Irrigon, Oregon, where they attend Columbia Junior High; and high schoolers from both Boardman and Irrigon attend Riverside High in Boardman.

The main problem currently facing the community is a lack of affordable housing for low-income families, according to city manager Allen. "Right now we're in the process of passing a new city ordinance that will call for opening up a larger section of the town to make room for affordable homes." There are no labor camps for migrant workers because the community does not have the resources to build them, Allen adds. Migrant workers who do come into the area find housing in a local trailer park or in apartment complexes. In one subdivision in the community, about 90 percent of the residents are Hispanics.

"The pressure for housing has increased tremendously. We are in desperate need for affordable, reasonable housing, but it's been real tough to do," Allen says. "One of the reasons is because many agriculture employers" have ignored "their responsibility. . . They think the people will just come in to work and then leave, but they don't think of housing them anywhere." Until the proposed city ordinance is passed or until funds are granted for building a labor camp, migrant workers must pay $200 to $300 a month for rent plus utilities.

Migrant Housing in Irrigon

Irrigon faces a similar quandary, made worse by the recent failure of a plan to develop low-income housing units. Some opponents of the project were concerned that it would create migrant housing, which they believe would devalue the character of the community—a quiet town of about 755 people. The project would have provided eight housing units on two parcels of land on Irrigon's south side. The plan was to build two-, three-, and four-bedroom units for lower-income families or individuals. The land was deeded to the city by Morrow County with the stipulation that it be used only for low-cost housing or it would revert back to county ownership.

The city had applied for $200,000 from the state Community Block Grant Program to pay for half of the development. No local tax monies were to be used. The development would have been owned by the Community Action Program of the East Central Oregon Association of Counties. Under the plan, families with at least one member who derived income from a farm-related activity would have received priority in the renting of the eight units. But a petition opposing the plan drew 200 signatures, nixing the proposal at the end of August 1991.

However, it is not a dead issue. Irrigon Mayor Don Eppenbach said the project will resurface. But in the meantime, migrant families in the area have to settle for living in rows of tiny houses cramped together on the outskirts of Irrigon or seven miles down the road in Umatilla.

"It's just plain discrimination," says Dan Hernandez of Boardman. Hernandez is executive director of La Causa, an organization formed to provide a voice for local Hispanics. "It's funny how people in the community are concerned about having migrant workers come into the area to harvest their crops, yet they don't care about where or how they live." Hernandez says that one of the major misconceptions held by the general public is that migrants are used to living under deplorable conditions. "They can't understand that these people have homes, nice homes, in Texas or wherever their home base is. But when they travel the road looking for work, then having to look for housing, they're really at the mercy of landlords."

"They think we're used to living 15 to a house and all sleeping on floors," says one woman in Spanish who asked not to be identified. "We're not. But when there is nothing else, what else can we do? And who do we go to for help?" This question is one asked by migrant workers around the nation; yet families who have traveled the country for many years in search of work still face the same problem—inadequate housing.

The National Picture

Many organizations and groups have been formed to combat the issue. But in many cases this has been to no avail.

"The biggest problem facing America today is. . .the threat of the homeless. The United States is in a crisis when it comes to housing and health," says Rafael Martinez, executive director of the North County Chaplaincy in Encinitas, California. The chaplaincy finds and provides adequate housing for those in need. "There are two types of homeless: those who live in the inner cities, who are usually mentally ill or drug and alcohol addicts, and the working/productive homeless from Mexico and Central America who will do the work that others won't do."

Martinez has spent the six years since his organization was formed traveling throughout the country—including visits to Walla Walla and Milton-Freewater—surveying the conditions in which migrant people live.

"They live in subhuman conditions, almost like animals," Martinez says. In San Diego County, "people will live in the mountains in makeshift houses constructed of cardboard because they cannot afford housing. When rent is $550 a month for one room with a small kitchen, or $700 a month for a two-room apartment, who can possibly afford something like that?" he asks.

Carlos Diaz, executive director of the Washington State Migrant Council in Sunnyside, notes that many migrants today live in the same housing conditions as they did in the 1950s. "They live under bridges or maybe one-room shacks. With the money they earn, they can't afford adequate housing, much less their own place."

Diaz estimates that there are 30,000 farm workers and 10,000 migrant families in the Yakima Valley. Although figures aren't available on how many of those live in substandard housing, Diaz says that too often "when they do find housing, these places are usually filled with rats and rodents. Or they have one hole in the ground for cooking and another hole in the ground that they use for a toilet."

Both Diaz and Martinez say the farm labor camp in Walla Walla, which is run by the county housing authority, and the camp in Milton-Freewater, which is operated by a non-profit corporation, are a lot better than housing projects available to migrant farm workers elsewhere. The two housing projects "are the best you'll ever see," says Martinez. But the camps aren't enough to fill the needs of the migrant work force that flocks to the Walla Walla Valley each year. The Walla Walla Farm Labor Camp, for example, filled its licensed capacity of 750 early in 1991. Privately owned rental housing was hard to find. A housing-shortage epidemic didn't materialize, but the influx of migrant workers and the local homeless population was enough to prompt local officials to consider housing people in tents the following year.

The housing situation to the north, in Columbia County, also is tight. At one town hall meeting in Dayton in June, Jim Nelson, plant manager for Pillsbury-Green Giant, said housing conditions were deplorable. Nelson said he knew of one case where 15 migrant workers were crowded into a basement apartment that had one bath and five beds.

In Idaho, the migrant camps usually consist of old army barracks that have been converted to studio apartments, according to Steve Citron, administrator of federal programs for the Idaho Housing Agency in Boise. "When you talk about 'single room occupancy' that means it doesn't necessarily have to have a bathroom or a kitchen," Citron says. "This usually means that the farm workers have to cook in community kitchens and use community bathrooms. This does not constitute comfortable or adequate housing."

With the problem of inadequate housing comes the additional problem of health care. Experts say that the two go hand-in-hand. "Without adequate housing one cannot have adequate health care. When you have eight people crowded into a two-bedroom apartment, that causes mental stress," claims Guillermo Castaneda, executive director of La Clinica Medical Center in Pasco. "There is also the issue of living with roaches, rats, and other rodents."

Diaz also says that children's self-esteem is lowered when they live under deplorable conditions. "They accept their substandard home – they begin to believe that that is the only way they can and will ever live, and they begin to feel ashamed. It's traumatic for a child to be afraid to bring their friends home because they are embarrassed of where they live."

In order for decent, safe, and sanitary housing to be made available to agricultural workers, advocates say the public's attitude needs to change. "Many sections of the Northwest are heavily dependent on migrant workers," according to Castaneda. "In Washington alone, about 23,000 to 24,000 units of housing are needed to address the migrant farm workers."

"But we need to stop thinking of these people as 'farm workers,'" Martinez says. "These people are the ones who put the food on our tables. The ones that are willing to work from sunup to sundown for $4.25 an hour."

"People who walk the streets and shop in your stores therefore pump money into the local economy," Castaneda adds.

Martinez notes that more people are becoming aware there is a problem, and that the time has come to do something about it. One positive step occurred recently in Oregon, for example, when the state government allotted $6,000,000 in federal funds to be spent on three- and four-bedroom housing units designated for migrant worker use during the next 10 years.

"We need to find decent housing for the people who feed our families. We need to develop a national agenda where housing and health are the priority, and now is the time to get this message to the president and Congress," concludes Martinez.

Raul Martinez begins work at dawn in a potato field near Boardman, Oregon. *Isabel Valle*

Temporary work; Raul and fellow worker Oziel Cerda removing shingles from the roof of a Walla Walla home. *Jeff Horner*

Raul and Maria Elena Martinez pose in their apartment doorway in Walla Walla, Washington, with sons (l. to r.) Jimmy, Billy, and Charlie. *Jeff Horner*

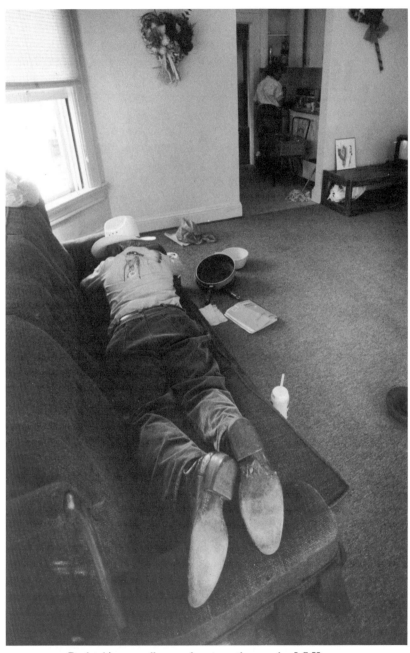

Raul taking a well earned rest on the couch. *Jeff Horner*

Working as a Walla Walla YWCA recreational aid, fifteen-year-old Charlie Martinez explains the rules of the game "Mr. Freeze" to a youngster during a Fun Factory outing to the Waitsburg, Washington, city park. *Jeff Horner*

Hired under the Try-Out Youth Employment program, seventeen-year-old Jaime Garcia pins on name tag before reporting to work at a Walla Walla area Pizza Hut. *Jeff Horner*

Maria Elena Martinez slices zucchini in the empty apartment in Boardman. *Isabel Valle*

Raul picking apples in an orchard near Boardman. *U-B Photo*

Migrant housing in Umatilla, Oregon. *Isabel Valle*

On the road to Texas; stopped with engine trouble near Green River, Utah. *Isabel Valle*

Chapter 3

Children in the Fields

A Summary of Washington State's Agricultural Child Labor Laws:

• Before employing minors, the employer must obtain written permission from a minor's parents and school.
• For every four hours worked, there is a 10-minute paid rest break; for more than five hours worked, there is a 30-minute meal period.
• The minimum age for most agricultural work is 14. Children 12 and 13 can work only during non-school weeks for hand-harvesting or cultivating berries, bulbs, cucumbers, and spinach.
• Children ages 12 and 13 may work only eight hours a day and 40 hours a week in non-school weeks, and begin no earlier than 5 a.m. and finish no later than 9 p.m.
• Children ages 14 and 15 may work up to 21 hours a week. This can include up to three hours a day before or after school, and eight hours a day on weekends. They may start work no earlier than 7 a.m. and finish no later than 8 p.m. on school days. Dairy, livestock, or daily irrigation work are exceptions. Work may begin at 6 a.m.
• When school is not in session, children ages 14 and 15 may work eight hours a day, 40 hours a week between the hours of 5 a.m. and 9 p.m.
• For minors 16 and 17, up to four hours a day of work before or after school is permitted, and up to 28 hours per week. When school is not in session, hours increase to 10 hours a day, 50 hours a week. Work cannot begin earlier than 5 a.m. and can finish no later than 10 p.m. and no later than 9 p.m. on two consecutive nights preceding a school day.
• All agricultural workers, including minors, must be paid the state minimum wage of $4.25, unless they are employed as hand-harvest labors and are paid on a piece rate.

THE ISSUE OF MINORS doing farm work is an emotional one that has caused great controversy between farmers, farm worker advocates, and even the parents of migrant children. There's been concern that depriving young workers of an adequate education perpetuates a cycle of poverty. Yet some migrant families depend on income from their children. In July 1990, following action by the state legislature, the Washington State Department of Labor and Industries adopted a set of agricultural child-labor rules that went into effect in November 1990. These rules are different than rules governing children in non-agricultural employment.

According to Roland Lund, spokesman with the Department of Labor and Industries in Olympia: "In 1990, the agricultural child labor laws were brought under the umbrella of all child labor laws. Before then, they were not covered. Children working in the fields were really not covered under any such laws."

The most significant difference between the new agricultural and non-agricultural child labor rules is that youths under the age of 16 are limited to a maximum of 18 hours of work during school weeks in non-agricultural jobs, while those employed in agricultural jobs may work as many as 21 hours a week. Another difference is that in non-agricultural employment, minors may work no more than five days in any one week, while agricultural child-labor laws state that no minor can be employed for more than six days in any one week.

"The bulk of the rules are pretty standard. They don't prohibit a child from working," says Carlos Reyes, safety inspector with the Washington State Department of Labor and Industries in Kennewick. Reyes further adds that the rules were adopted after six to eight months of extensive research and interviews with government officials, representatives of migrant workers, and school officials: "These new rules are structured to encourage school attendance and still get in a good amount of hours worked."

Agricultural employers not in compliance with the rules may be penalized up to $250 per violation. "So far, the compliance rate has been very low and that is a major concern to us," Lund says. "Since the rules went into effect in November 1990, 1,411 of the approximately 10,000 agricultural employers in the state of Washington have obtained minor work permits. Yet we know there are a lot more agricultural employers who do hire minors to work in the fields." Lund said his office would attempt that winter to find out why agricultural employers are not complying with the new laws. "It might be that they just need some educating on the new laws. So that is one of the things we hope to accomplish this winter and therefore prepare them for next harvest season."

In the state of Oregon, child labor laws governing all types of employment are much more relaxed. According to the Oregon Bureau of

Labor and Industries, Wage and Hour Division, children as young as 9 may work on a small farm and get paid the state's minimum wage of $4.75 an hour. Minors who are 16 and 17 are no longer restricted to work within specific hours. They may work up to any time of the day or night and up to 44 hours per week.

Although the Washington rules are set up to protect children, some advocates say the laws should specifically prohibit them from working before school and others say children should be excluded altogether from farm labor. Citing statistics revealing that 86 percent of Washington's farm worker children do not graduate from high school, Sam Martinez of the Washington State Migrant Council in Sunnyside believes that no school-age children should work in the fields before classes. This exclusion would effectively prevent children from involvement in labor-intensive work like asparagus picking. Martinez also suggested that students should be required to maintain a minimum "C" grade point average before they are allowed to do farm work.

Dr. Don Gargas, a pediatrician at the Yakima Valley Farm Workers Clinic in Toppenish, notes that agricultural work is the nation's most dangerous occupation and that 300 children die in accidents each year on farms across the nation. "Many of the accidents are the result of carelessness that is the result of immaturity," says Gargas, who is opposed to having children working in the fields. "Not all injuries are fatal," he adds. "I see a lot with sore backs, sore wrists, and lacerations from cutting asparagus."

Kids in the Fields: What's the Harm?

Maria Elena has seen the physical ailments field work produces in children; she also has much to say about its long-term effects. "Child labor laws. They should do away with kids working in the fields altogether," she complains in Spanish.

The 52-year-old mother of 13 says that as a result of her children working in the fields year-round, three of her five youngest have been kept a year behind in school. "The kids have to be in the fields as of 4 a.m., which means they have to get up around 3 a.m. Then from the fields they go to school. Well, how can they do it? They all fall asleep in class."

In 1990, one of her sons, Robert, 19, along with a dozen or so other migrant students, was employed in the asparagus harvest in Boardman. Their daily working days began at 4 a.m. and continued until noon or 3 p.m. After they left the fields, they returned home to take showers, get something to eat, and immediately went to school for three hours of intensive study.

"The kids were always asleep. How could they concentrate in their studies after being up since 3 a.m. and working all day in the hot sun without any breaks?" Maria Elena asks. "And asparagus is the worst because you have to be out there in the morning to cut them, not after school." Although school children in Boardman no longer work in asparagus fields (which were plowed under following the harvest), minors continue working in agriculture while they are going to school. One school official who mentors migrant students here says there are at least seven minors, two who are 15 years old, working in the fields from 4 p.m. to midnight every day.

"We became aware of this because their teacher kept noticing that they were falling asleep in class," says the official, who asked to remain anonymous for fear of retaliation. The parents of one of the children claimed their child came home from work at 9 p.m. The child, however, when confronted earlier by officials, had admitted he had been out working until midnight. "Parents have to lie in order for their children to continue working because the family depends on the child's income," the school official states.

The school has the authority to step in to require that a child not work long hours in order to get adequate sleep and therefore function properly in school. But, according to the school official, Boardman schools "will go after 'settled out migrants' that they see have potential, but they really won't go after migrant students that will be leaving in a couple of months or so. And is that really fair? No." (A "settled out migrant" is someone who used to travel the country in search of farm work, but now remains in the same location on a year-round basis. A "migrant student" is one who continues moving with his family throughout the country on a regular basis.)

Principal Dave Youngbluth of Boardman's Riverside High says the school is interested in getting all children enrolled in classes, regardless of whether they are agricultural workers or not. "If we know of any migrant student—settled-out migrant or not—that is not in school, then we will approach the parents and inform them that we will take legal action if their child is not in school. It is a state law that any child under the age of 16 is required to go to school and we comply with that law."

Youngbluth adds, "As for children age 16 and older, they are not restricted to work under specific hours. But if they work during school hours, they must first have mutual consent from the parents as well as the school. We won't pull them off the job but we will go speak with their parents. Currently, we are in the process of getting one 17-year-old back to school."

Although migrant high school students in Walla Walla do not work the fields in October, they are employed in the canneries at that time. "We have one young man who is currently working from 2 p.m. to 10 p.m. and is trying to work his school schedule around those hours," says Sergio Hernandez, bilingual coordinator at the high school. "He's doing very well in school but he also has to work hard to help support his family here and in Mexico."

The Walla Walla and Boardman high schools both have Cooperative Work Experience programs, whereby students are taken out of the fields and placed in other places of employment in the community, such as in restaurants or grocery stores. "The pressure to work is tremendous, but we try to keep them in school. So we try to put them in other jobs where their studies won't be affected," Hernandez says.

Maria Elena believes such programs are aimed at helping migrant students, but her continuous plea is to eliminate all children from working in the fields. "The migrant kids, the ones that move from place to place — not the ones that are settled in one town — those are the ones that no one pays attention to," she says. "In the schools they just pass them because they are too old. You should see how many migrant kids in Texas finish without knowing anything."

Maria Elena's concerns are voiced by many other migrants as well as educators, and in response the federal government has initiated programs supporting migrant children's education. Some of these programs, like the Texas Migrant Council, take education to the student; others, like the Pendleton Migrant Education Program and the Boardman Child Development Center, take the student to education. In most cases, this means teaching English to Spanish-speaking children.

Pendleton Migrant Education Program

A 6-year-old child walks into a classroom in Boardman for his first day of school. He's nervous because there are no familiar faces around him. Within a few minutes the teacher walks in and starts talking. The rest of the class responds to what the teacher is saying, except for that little boy. He doesn't understand what the teacher is saying. While the teacher is speaking English, the little boy understands only Spanish.

But today, that child and others like him have a chance to succeed in school because of a program offered through the Umatilla Educational Service District's Migrant Education Program, in Pendleton, Oregon. Officials there say the migrant student dropout rate in Morrow and Umatilla counties is about 30 percent, compared with a national average of 80 percent, thanks to the program the ESD operates. Officials attribute that success to the one-on-one attention teachers give pupils, and because many migrant students in the two counties come from families who have settled in the area; thus the youngsters are not constantly moving from one school to another.

The program, called Chapter 1, originated two decades ago when the federal government realized there was a need to provide children with special assistance. It allocates funds to aid any student who needs special help in developing math and reading skills, or who may have been kept behind one year in school. Some funds in Chapter 1 are set aside for the "Chapter 1 Migrant" program. In this case, federal funds are funnelled through the state, says Kay Fenimore-Smith, director of the migrant education program for ESD. The office serves 11 school districts in Umatilla and Morrow counties; the migrant program involves 25 schools in eight targeted districts throughout the two counties.

"The purpose of this program is to help kids make it in school," Fenimore-Smith notes. "The funds are used for instructional purposes and for support purposes such as translation, making sure their immunization records are in order, and for home visits."

Under the "Chapter 1 Migrant" program, teachers determine whether children enrolled in school need special assistance in vocabulary. If so, they are placed in the program. At the elementary level, the student will leave the classroom for special assistance up to 1½ hours a day. "This is done so they can primarily learn English. Otherwise, we really try to keep them in the classrooms because mainstreaming is better for the child," Fenimore-Smith says. At the high school level, students receive special help for one or two periods a day.

In Boardman, Lisa Constantine and her assistant, Christine Garcia, head the program for migrant children. Daily exercises usually include learning the basics of English through reading, talking, and other activities such as drawing and coloring, which help the child to put words to pictures. These instructors work closely with the homeroom teachers to make sure the students are up-to-date with the lessons taught to the rest of the class. Sometimes, story books are read in Spanish to make the children feel at home and more at ease. And when necessary, instructions are given in Spanish to make sure a child understands; otherwise, English is heard most often.

"We work closely with these kids and we try to get them to the level that they should be. Working with these students, you see that if they're behind it's usually because of the language barrier," Constantine points out. "Also, the majority of the students we have come directly from Mexico. And what they teach over there is different from our curriculum, so of course they are behind."

In past years, the migrant education program has proved to be so successful that some students have continued on to college. "This year we have two students attending colleges in Idaho under full scholarships. And two other students had [so much] initiative and drive to continue their education that they applied for grants. They, too, are attending college," Fenimore-Smith says.

But even with a high success rate and a program that has proven effective, the ESD faced difficulty the past few years: namely, insufficient funds. "In 1987, we had 1,125 students in the migrant program." In 1990, "that number increased to 1,579. In terms of dollars per student in 1987 it was $620 per student and in 1990 that amount decreased to $457," notes Fenimore-Smith. "Nationally, funds have increased, but it hasn't kept up with the number of pupils."

Also, rules for the program have changed. A few years ago, it served students from grades 1 through 12. Now, the program includes preschoolers. "And, a large portion of migrant children are preschoolers and elementary students."

Until more federal funds can be allotted to the program, the instructors have to find creative ways to reach more children. Some parents of preschoolers, for example, are given mimeographed pages that include basic English lessons covering colors, the alphabet, and numbers. The pamphlet, in Spanish and English, instructs parents to teach preschoolers in the home, and parents are given monthly training in the use of the pamphlets. "The ideal situation would be to place the child in an institutional setting. But since we don't have the resources available, we have to do with what we have," exclaims Fenimore-Smith.

Texas Migrant Council

Texas Migrant Council workers have traveled the nation for more than 20 years helping young migrant children from their state to learn the alphabet and direct them in preschool activities. Administrators, teachers, nurses, cooks, bus drivers, and other Migrant Council staff members have taken on the role of migrants themselves, as they packed up their belongings each spring and headed off to different parts of the country.

But the Texas Migrant Council tradition is coming to an end. Beginning in the spring of 1992, TMC staff members will be traveling less and less as other states develop their own Migrant Headstart programs, which will include children from Texas. Agencies in most of the 30 states where the TMC employees have traveled—including Washington—say they will be able to make a smooth transition. The planned change, however, worries some parents who were previously secure in the knowledge that their children were being looked after by familiar faces.

TMC staff members have helped children ages 2 to 6 learn their numbers, the alphabet, colors, and in some cases words, in both Spanish and English. "Our staff are like migrants themselves. Every year we close down here in Texas and everyone packs their bags and follows the children to where their parents travel," says Jamie Ramirez, TMC center director in LaGrulla. But the federal government, which pays for the relocation, is asking other states to help because the cost of moving the Texas centers has become too expensive.

There are 47 TMC centers throughout Texas. More than half are located in the South Texas Valley, which is where most migrant families are from. There are 600 employees. The centers serve about 3,750 children, notes Oscar Villerreal, executive director of the Texas Migrant Council. He estimates that 1,179 of them travel each spring to Washington state, primarily to the Yakima Valley. Villerreal points out that the history of the TMC centers relocating to other states dates back to the 1960s, "when we found out that some of these states that the families were traveling to did not have services for migrant children."

Ramirez has been traveling with LaGrulla families during the harvest season since 1969. In the past, he has set up centers in Grandview, Prosser, Basin City, and Eltopia. In 1991, about 550 children traveled with their parents from LaGrulla to Basin City and Eltopia, while about 100 staff members from various TMC centers, including the 11 employees from LaGrulla, made the trip in seven buses.

"It's been pretty hard on the staff, because many leave their families behind. Then when they get to these locations they have to find housing and start a whole new life there," Ramirez says. Compensation is low, too. Employees receive minimum wage, and they have to pay for half of the relocation costs out of their own pocket. This spring, most of that traveling will end, and state governments will have to provide the services that TMC has been providing.

"There were two reasons for this move. One, the government feels it's 'old fashioned'; and second, but most importantly, it is not cost-effective," Villerreal says. TMC is a federally funded program that cost $250,000 the first year that the centers were relocated. "This past year. . .the federal government funded us at $13.2 million." Program costs have increased as more parents each year place their children at TMC centers rather than take them into the fields, Villerreal says.

He points out that some states are unhappy with their new responsibilities: "I think we will have to return to Indiana, Wisconsin, and Ohio this coming spring, because those states do not have the capability to handle our children." States assuming responsibility include Washington, Kansas, Michigan, and Oklahoma. Two decades ago, TMC opened a seasonal center in Oregon. But now the Texas workers do not have to return, because Oregon has begun its own Migrant Headstart programs for migrants' children.

Tina Kroth, Washington State Migrant Council's administrative assistant in Sunnyside, says Washington does not foresee any problems in serving the 1,000 or more Texas migrant children. "We're always prepared. We'll be able to provide them with the same type of quality care that they've always had and that we give our own children." However, she would not talk about any specific plans her agency has because it hadn't received confirmation from the federal government that the change will take place.

Now, the TMC centers will remain open 10 months each year in Texas, closing in July and August. "We do have some children that remain in the area, but only about 40," says Livia Cantu, the head teacher at the LaGrulla center. "Yet, I'm looking forward to staying here because it got tiresome after a while."

Villerreal and Cantu said parents of migrant children seem concerned, however. "They want to know if their child is going to get the same type of service that we gave them. For example, since they were our kids we sometimes drove our buses 50 miles to go pick up a child and bring him to the center," Cantu says. "They want to know if the same thing is going to be done next year."

"The parents are concerned, but I can almost guarantee that if people are not doing their jobs, we are sure going to hear about it," Villerreal said.

Boardman Child Development Center

Raul and Maria Elena share the concerns of other migrant parents. For the Martinezes, education is the top priority for their children. Although the family usually begins the trek north in mid-March and does not return to Texas until October or November, the children don't suffer from lack of schooling. The three youngest—Billy, Jimmy and Charlie—have attended schools in Texas, Washington, and Oregon within one school year. They are placed in schools immediately upon arrival in a new community. One day after the family moved to Boardman, for example, Billy was enrolled in the local child development center which serves both migrant and non-migrant children. Charlie, meanwhile, works in the fields to generate needed income before enrolling in high school in the fall in Boardman or Texas. Jimmy is too old for the child development center, but does spend his afternoons at the local public library.

The Martinezes find the center an ideal place for Billy. Notes Janie Swann, the center's director and head teacher: "The purpose of the center is to provide a clean, well balanced educational program, give quality care, proper nutrition, rest time, and to help the child adjust to new concepts and ideas. Therefore, the constant moving will not affect them as much."

The Boardman Child Development Center also offers parenting classes and in-home visits. The center is licensed by Oregon's Children's Services Division. Funds are generated through a minimal tuition fee and two grants awarded annually by Morrow County. One grant is for migrant education.

Parents of migrant children pay $1 per week for each child who attends the center. "This rate is based on 1989-1990 state statistics that indicate the average income for agricultural workers is $8,700 a year for a household of 4.7," Swann explains. "For this reason, parents only pay $1 a week to bring their child in." The center operates five days a week. "We have the capacity to attend to 38 children ages 3 through 12, but this summer has been very slow. One week we may only have four [migrant] children, plus about eight non-migrants."

One of the main reasons for the low number of migrant children attending this summer is the lack of work for farm workers. "We're agriculture-based, but this year [Morrow] county was harvesting non-migrant crops," explains Swann. Farmers reduced the amount of labor-intensive crops that were planted—such as beans or onions—so that they wouldn't have to hire as many migrant workers. "For example, wheat is all done with combines." Consequently, there was not enough work in the fields for both parents from a migrant family in the early part of the summer—so more children were staying at home with their mothers. "So where we would normally have 12 migrant children in our center, this time we only had four," says Swann.

Even with the small number of children attending the center, Swann and her staff of three assistants and one part-time worker are kept busy providing activities for the children, including arts and crafts, and preparing a nutritional meal and two snacks a day. In addition to the migrant children, non-migrant children whose parents work in the local plants also attend. Parents of non-migrant children pay $1.50 an hour to enroll their children in the center.

Integrating migrant children with non-migrant children is also a major purpose of the center. This allows the children to learn from each other as they become aware of cultural differences. And most importantly, it allows Spanish-speaking children to practice their English and therefore grow up fluent in both languages. The Martinezes see two advantages to sending Billy to the center. First, says Raul, Billy is able to be with other children his age. Secondly, says Maria, it keeps him used to the idea of being in an educational environment, which will help when school resumes.

Swann would like to offer those benefits on a greater scale to migrant workers and their families. "There is a lot of need for this center, and the ideal situation for me would be to have it opened six to seven days a week, all shifts, but I haven't generated enough support," Swann notes.

Chapter 4
Family Ties

THERE IS A certain stigma attached to the words "migrant worker," a stigma that in many cases has arisen from misconceptions, misinformation, or a lack of knowledge. When a community that is predominantly Caucasian is faced with a group of people who are different not only in color, but also in language and culture, difficulties may arise. In order for both groups to get along, understanding must first be developed. The established community is dealing not only with a group of people who have a different lifestyle, but also a different culture and way of thinking.

First of all, migrants who come to the Pacific Northwest year after year in search of farm work are primarily of Hispanic origin. Whether they be from Mexico, Central America, South America, or are U.S. citizens of Mexican descent, it's important to understand the Hispanic lifestyle. The major difference is family unity. In Hispanic households, female children remain in their parents' homes until they are married. When the women marry, they live with their in-laws. Therefore, the number of people living under one roof expands.

Large families are also traditional among Hispanics, especially among Hispanic migrants. Take, for example, the Martinezes, who have 13 children. Maria Elena wanted a large number of children because that means more household income once the children are old enough to work, which is usually at the age of 10. Maria Elena also says she had lots of children so she would have someone to look after her and her husband once they are older, or if they are sick. "I don't want to be put in a nursing home," she says. It is also common for the older children to stay at home and look after the younger ones while the parents are at work.

Hispanic migrant families are a closely united group because they are all they have. It is hard for people to establish any type of relationships with other people when they are never in one place for long. Therefore, the relationships they do establish are within their own group. Often times when they marry, they will marry other migrants—so the cycle never ends.

They are also quick to lend a helping hand to other migrant families. It is not uncommon to share food, clothes, or even lodging. When one member of a migrant household comes home with a sack of potatoes, tomatoes, apples, or onions, it is shared equally with other nearby families. And if someone has no place to sleep, others will always open a door even if their household is already crowded with people.

"You always have to think of others who have less than you do," Maria Elena says. "We may be poor, but we have a lot more than other people, so we share what we do have."

Migrants are a proud and conscientious people as well. Because of limited incomes, they are careful to purchase only what they need. Yet, should an emergency arise and purchases have to be made on credit, they never forget their debts. This year the Martinezes have been paying off bills that accumulated the previous year when they needed medical care and four tires for their truck. Consequently, they have been receiving notices from collection agencies.

"We know we're late in our payments, but what can we do when we have no money?" Raul explains. "I hate to owe anywhere, but the only thing I can do is work and pay off those bills a little at a time."

"They may not get their money immediately, but we never forget where we owe and we will make sure we pay off our bills," Maria Elena adds. True to their word, the family recently drove into Pendleton and handed over about $50 to the collection agency, the final payment on their bills.

One perception in the community is that it is typical for Hispanic men to talk among themselves in a closed group while sitting on the front lawn or gathered around a car or truck, looking under the hood. Since money is scarce and mechanics are expensive, they try to find ways of fixing cars themselves. This is when they have the time to discuss such topics as work, family, and the high cost of living—a way of unwinding, or relaxing over a cold beer. The women are usually inside cooking, sharing recipes, or talking about children. Since money is scarce, it is very rare for the children to enjoy a day out at the theater, at the mall, or even at a school athletic activity. They find ways of entertaining themselves at home with their relatives or friends.

With a little understanding of differences in culture and lifestyle, one can understand why these people live in crowded conditions under one roof, why they may be seen standing around a car drinking beer, or why they have so many children. A closer look at the Martinezes — and at one of their children in particular — reveals the tight-knit nature of the migrant family.

The Martinez "Support Network"

Since the Martinezes arrived in Boardman, there has been an instant bonding between the family and its extended members. On the day the family arrived, Raul's eldest son, Raul Jr., went looking for work for his father. Their daughter-in-law, Iris, asked her friends to see if anyone had extra furniture that they could lend the family. Iris also took it upon herself to make sure Billy was enrolled in the local child development center. The women of the family share the responsibility of looking after the children. They sometimes cooperate in preparing meals, and more often than not share cooking utensils and other household supplies.

Frequently found sitting at the breakfast, lunch, or dinner table are family members who may not live under the same roof, or friends and neighbors who have dropped by for a visit. The happiest moments of the day seem to be the evenings after dinner. Everyone will normally gather at the Martinez apartment to watch television, or to discuss family issues and share stories. Sometimes the Bible is read and discussed, and other times everyone sits outside and splits open a watermelon for all to eat.

"We're a very close family and we believe in looking out for one another. Each one of my children care and look after each other. They all believe in working and I've never had any problems with anyone of them before," Maria Elena says proudly.

Each member of the Martinez family plays a distinct role. Each has his or her own responsibilities and position in the household. Raul is the breadwinner — and that's what he lives for. Work is his priority because he is responsible for feeding, clothing, and housing his family. Although he works long, hard hours in the fields, usually from 6 a.m. to 6 p.m. under the hot sun, Raul is never in a foul mood when he walks through the door in the evening. As a matter of fact, there is a little spring in his walk and a look of satisfaction painted on his face. On payday, Raul and Maria Elena go over the family expenses and the budgeting starts. There is food to buy, rent and utilities to pay, school clothes to purchase.

Maria Elena is a housewife. At 52, and after rearing 10 other children, she still has the stamina to look after her three youngest kids. She wakes up at 3:30 a.m. to prepare breakfast and lunch for Raul and Charlie. After they leave for work at 5:30 a.m., Maria Elena sometimes takes a quick nap. Then it's up again at 8 a.m. to have breakfast ready for the two younger children. Her days are filled with cleaning the apartment, washing loads of clothes, ironing and folding clothes, cooking, grocery shopping, visiting the local post office, and entertaining friends and neighbors who come to visit. She also makes sure the boys keep up with their studies even when they are not in school.

"I love to keep busy. I can't find myself just sitting around; I guess it's because I'm used to it," Maria Elena says.

Charlie

Both Raul and Maria Elena work hard — and that mentality has passed on to their children. It is definitely seen in Charlie. When Charlie is not at school, he works alongside his father in the fields. For a 15-year-old, Charlie has taken on the responsibility of an adult, and in many respects he is treated as an adult. He too wakes up at 4:30 or 5 a.m. and prepares for a long, hard day. When he is in the fields he works just as his father does. And as the hours and days start taking their toll on him, Raul repeatedly keeps telling him in Spanish, "Come on, don't be lazy. You have to keep working."

When Charlie comes home from work, he too is treated as the man of the house. For example, he is seated at the dinner table next to his father and immediately served. Upon his arrival home from work, looking tired, he usually makes some remark about how he hates to labor in the fields. But after a hot meal and a quick shower he won't mention it again. Charlie plays the role of an adult in other respects as well. He helps his father with the truck's upkeep, looks after his younger brothers when his parents are not around, and he's the navigator when the family is on the road. Payday for Charlie is a big event. He eagerly tears open his check and quickly adds up the money he's earned to pay for school clothes.

The issue that constantly occupies Charlie's mind, however, is going home to Texas. This is his first priority, and the question lingers in his mind day and night. Since the first day I moved in with the family, almost two months ago, that's all I've heard Charlie ask his parents. Now that school is right around the corner, that question is heard even more.

Maria Elena and Raul have decided to enroll their two youngest children at the local elementary school here, as they did last year. But with Charlie it's a different story. He will be a freshman this year and says he wants to go to school in Texas. It must be hard for a 15-year-old to be separated from his buddies at a time when their companionship is very important and vital to him. And the rest of his family — brothers and sisters, uncles, aunts, cousins, and grandparents — are all back in Texas. I once asked Charlie if he liked the communities he has lived in and if he liked traveling. He responded, "Yeah, I like traveling. The only thing is, that wherever we travel to it only means work."

My heart aches for him every morning at 4 a.m. when Raul and Maria Elena start pleading with Charlie to wake up to go work. When he finally gets up, he staggers around, until sitting down at the table and dropping his head on folded arms. With enough prodding, Charlie finally does walk out the door, heading to the fields with his father.

"I feel so sorry for him; he's so young and yet he works so hard," his mother will say throughout the day. And when Charlie returns home from work, the first thing he'll ask is, "When are we going home?" There is always dead silence from his parents, although sometimes his mother will tell Charlie to be quiet and his father gets angry with him.

But going home seems to be in Maria Elena's mind as well. "It's hard to be separated from your children," she'll say. Raul and Maria Elena have nine other children in Texas, and since they left home they have had two new grandsons. So far, Raul and Maria Elena know them only through photos. The Martinezes' two youngest children never ask about returning home. Jimmy says he likes Boardman and that only once in a while he longs for Texas.

As for Raul, his main concern is whether he will find work, and if so, where. He's currently hoeing fields of onions, potatoes, and other crops, but that work will probably end this week. Meanwhile, the evenings are filled with discussions on how to send Charlie back to Texas. Do we look for a ride for him with a family friend who is already returning to Texas? Do we send him on the bus? If so, when? And Charlie's days are filled with hoeing fields from 6 a.m. to 6 p.m., wondering when all this will end.

Cutting the Apron Strings

It takes a lot of courage and drive for a 15-year-old to leave his parents behind and travel several thousand miles to return to his hometown for school. For the first time in his life, Charlie has decided to cut the apron strings. He will be taking a bus to LaGrulla in order to start his freshman year at Rio Grande High School. He plans to live with an older brother and sister until his parents return later in the fall. Consequently, on Monday afternoon, August 19, with one suitcase in hand and a few last-minute carry-ons, Charlie boards a Greyhound bus, prepared for the four-day trip that will take him to the southernmost tip of Texas.

"I don't want him to go, but this is something he's been wanting for so long that I have to let him go," Maria Elena says. Charlie's older brother, Robert, had left the family last year so he too could return to Texas in time for school to start. But Robert was 17; Charlie is only 15.

"I'm scared to see him travel by himself. So is Raul. But this is the only way he can get to Texas. So we'll just pray to God that he will be all right," his mother exclaims.

For weeks the family looked around for a friend who could possibly take Charlie to Texas, but they always came across obstacles. Families had already left, there was no room for him, or people were not leaving at the right time. Raul was more reluctant than Maria Elena to let Charlie spread his wings and fly the coop. But it was not so much a fear of letting Charlie travel alone, as it was that Charlie is his father's "right hand" man.

"I don't know why you're leaving, Charlie. Who's going to help me load and unload the truck [when we leave for Texas], and who's going to help me around here?" Raul asked, when Charlie made preparations to leave.

The fact that Charlie is returning to Texas ahead of the rest of the family is a major issue for the Martinezes. To the parents, it indicates that their son has grown up and is now making his own decisions. And, in a migrant family, it is very rare for a son who has a role as vital as Charlie's to be allowed to leave when there is still work available in the fields. Although Maria Elena does not want him to go, she realizes this is probably best for Charlie. "If I don't let him go he's just going to keep nagging me every day. But most importantly, his education will suffer."

"He's not going to want to pay attention in class, he won't study, he may even stop going to school. It's hard at that age to be taken out of schools and put into new schools. That happened to me and so I just stopped going to school. I don't want the same thing to happen to him. Education is something that is very important to us, and if this is what is going to make Charlie happy and keep him going to school, then we'll make the sacrifice and send him ahead of us."

Jimmy and Billy also gave their input regarding their older brother leaving. Teary-eyed, Jimmy complained to his parents that he, too, wanted to return to Texas to attend school. His parents tell him it is impossible to let him go because he needs to be with them. Charlie tried to comfort him: "Don't worry Jimmy, before you know it you'll be home too." Billy sadly looked down and said he will miss his brother.

Prior to his departure, Charlie fought playfully with his younger brothers, and many times he took them off to a corner to give them last-minute brotherly advice. "Jimmy, remember, don't go swimming unless there is a grownup with you."

Charlie's sister-in-law, Iris, living upstairs from the Martinezes, commented, "It's something to have that drive inside of you to make you want to leave so bad so you can start school in your own hometown."

Charlie contemplated what it would be like leaving his parents behind for the first time. "Pero que vale," he said after a while. "They'll be soon home."

The bus trip home will prove to be a maturing experience: a 68-hour, approximately 3,000 mile trip through Idaho, Utah, Colorado, New Mexico, and Texas. At the beginning of the trip, Charlie is a little reluctant to ask questions at the bus stations. But after a while he overcomes his shyness and begins asking Greyhound workers when the next bus will leave and when it is scheduled to arrive at a certain location. A little homesickness also sets in the first two days. But after calling his family and hearing his mother's voice at the other end of the line, his spirits perk up and he begins enjoying the long trip home.

However, spending the night on a cramped bus, resting his head on a window sill, is not the most comfortable way to sleep. "What time is it?" "What day is it?" "Where are we?" he asks, his eyes drowsy. As the bus makes its way from town to town, Charlie passes time looking out the window, taking in every site. His enthusiasm grows as the bus arrives in the big cities. His eyes widen when he sees the tall buildings in Salt Lake City and Denver, but he quickly points out that big cities are not for him. What he seems to enjoy most are the farm roads.

"That's a bean field, and that one over there is an onion field. They're growing corn here, and over there, potato," he says. Shortly, the focus turns to his hands. "How do you call these in English," as he points to callouses on his left hand. "I get those from working in the fields," he says proudly. "It's hard work."

Charlie has been working in the fields alongside his father for the past four years: "I don't like it," he points out. "But when there is nothing else, you have to go work in 'el labor.' I don't know if I'm going to continue doing this the rest of my life. I don't know what I'm going to do in my life. I've never, never, never thought about that."

To avoid further homesickness, Charlie talks about arriving home and what he is going to do instead of talking about the family he has left behind. "The first thing I'm going to do when I get there is rest, then the next day I'll go get my hair cut for school and I'll go shopping for clothes." From hoeing beans, potatoes, and onions in Boardman, Charlie has earned about $600.

"When I'm at home I am going to be responsible for waking up in the mornings and getting to school on time. I'll also help my sister with the house and I'll baby-sit all my nephews and nieces," he says. Charlie also comments: "My parents were scared to let me go by myself, and I was a little scared too. But now that I've done it I know I'll be able to travel by myself next year."

In LaGrulla, Charlie will be living with an older brother and sister and will also be looked after by other brothers, sisters, and other family members. The only difficulty they could face is if they are denied extra food stamps, a matter that hasn't been determined yet.

As the bus gets closer to Texas, Charlie's excitement grows stronger. "It's been five months since I left Texas. That's a long time." Along an eastern New Mexico highway a huge sign can be seen in the distance, and, as the bus draws nearer, Charlie reads out loud, "Welcome to Texas," and a slight smile forms on his lips. "When I come with my family we all cheer when we see that sign," he recalls. "I miss that."

About 20 hours later, the bus reaches LaGrulla, where one of his older sisters is waiting. "My you've grown," she says after they hug and kiss. "Later we'll go get your hair cut, and tomorrow we'll go shopping," she says. But before that, it is time to get reacquainted with family, friends, and the Texas heat.

Chapter 5

Health: Parasites, Heart Disease, and Malnutrition

RAUL WALKS AROUND the house with a distinct look of pain in his eyes. For days he hasn't talked much and he has made sure the foods he eats are soft to chew. Maria Elena says he has been complaining of a toothache for months, but hasn't wanted to see a dentist.

As the days go by the pain gets worse. Raul can be heard waking up various times throughout the night, pacing the floor and gargling with warm salt water. Twice he makes appointments with a dentist, but doesn't keep them. At the times he is scheduled to have his tooth pulled he is in the fields working—that is more important. It is not until the pain is too much to endure, and his wife is tired of seeing him walk around in pain, that Raul finally decides to take one day off from work and have the tooth pulled.

Maria Elena suffers from a bad back. She was injured last April when a drunken driver hit their truck from behind. Sometimes she finds it difficult to walk or sit, but she has not sought treatment. "I'm afraid to go to the doctor. I know they're going to charge me a lot of money and I don't have it," she says sadly.

Life without Medical Insurance

Although medical care is a priority for migrant laborers and their families, often it is hard for them to receive the assistance they need. According to recent medical studies conducted by the University of Texas Health Science Center in San Antonio, the life expectancy of a migrant is 48 years, and a 40-year-old male farm worker will have the same ailments as a 60-year-old non-migrant. The study also indicates that the woman in a migrant household will be the last to seek medical attention. The first priority is the children, then the husband, then the wife. There are two reasons for this: lack of money and constant relocating.

While working at Pasco and Walla Walla, the Martinezes received medical coupons from the Washington State Department of Social and Health Services for sons Charlie, Jimmy, and Billy. "Charlie needs a lot of work on his teeth and we had appointments with a dentist when we were in Pasco. But the appointments were during the day, Raul was always at work, and since I can't drive, I had no way of getting there," Maria Elena recalls. The coupons were never used and the children were never examined.

Laws differ from state to state, however. In Oregon, the only one in the family who is eligible for medical coupons is Billy, since only children aged 7 and younger receive assistance. When state health officials told the Martinezes in a letter that Billy had not had a medical or dental checkup in a long time, he was taken immediately to the nearest health clinic, in Hermiston, 25 miles away.

"It's hard for us because we've taken the children to the doctor before, but it always ends up costing us so much money. I'm not going to let my children get sick, so the only thing we can do when we see a doctor is arrange to pay in payments," Maria Elena says.

But the problem is twofold: not only is it difficult for a family to seek medical assistance, but once patients are treated, the biggest problem facing doctors and the medical community is contacting patients for follow-up procedures. This is a major concern for Dr. Ben Rodriguez, medical director of the Walla Walla Family Health Clinic: "For example, someone gets a physical and during the process they get a blood test. Then the next week they pick up and move. How does the doctor get in contact with them to let them know they need medical attention?"

Rodriguez believes a networking system should be developed within the medical community allowing for migrants' records to be transferred electronically from one clinic to another, depending on where families relocate. Right now the only thing that can be done is for migrants to take it upon themselves to return to a health clinic and obtain their test results. Then they must carry their medical records everywhere they go. But often this is hard to do, since it is not unusual for a family to pack up and leave on a day's notice.

Migrant workers suffer more often from medical and dental problems than other elements of society, according to research conducted at migrant health centers by the National Migrant Resource Program, Inc. Roberta Ryder, NMRP executive director, notes that in the migrant community there seems to be more cases of every illness, and health problems are allowed to progress to very serious stages.

"While the majority of medical conditions seen in migrant health centers are common, it is not unusual to encounter diseases that would be seen once in a lifetime, if ever, in other groups of the U.S. population," Ryder says. "Migrants not only live in Third World conditions, they are subjected to Third World diseases," such as parasitic diseases, amoebic liver conditions, salmonella, polio, and yellow fever.

In a 1990 nationwide study conducted at migrant health centers, migrants were asked to list the illnesses that had afflicted their families during 1989. The study, funded by the NMRP, was directed by Robert T. Trotter II of the Department of Anthropology at Northern Arizona University, Flagstaff, and Dr. Paul Monahan with the Yakima Valley Farm Workers' Clinic, Yakima. They found that some health problems—including diabetes, cardiovascular disease, and asthma—occur more frequently among migrant workers.

"The majority of migrants' health problems are identical to the health problems encountered in any poor population in the United States," Ryder says. "These are the illnesses which are caused by poor nutrition, lack of resources to seek care early in the disease process, accidents, exposure from hard manual labor, and infectious diseases from overcrowding and poor sanitation."

"I've been working with farm workers for the past 20 years and I can give you testimony from actual experience that migrant workers suffer more from these illnesses than the general public," Monahan points out. "We have a lot of information, but there aren't a lot of detailed studies where we can actually compare the migrant population to the non-migrant population," he notes. "All I can say is that migrant clinics see patients for these illnesses more often than clinics for the general public do."

Monahan notes that up to 78 percent of all farm workers—in contrast to two or three percent of the general public—suffer from parasitic infection. He adds that the death rates for farm workers from influenza and pneumonia are 20 percent and 200 percent higher, respectively, than the national average. As most migrant women do not receive prenatal care, there is a high incidence of premature deliveries and other birth complications. In addition, high risk pregnancies are frequent, occurring among both very young and much older women.

According to the study, migrants also identify and treat some medical conditions as simple ailments, but these actually are symptoms for other underlying illnesses. These would be identified as the more serious health problems that they actually are if they were observed by health professionals. One reason migrants tend to administer treatment to themselves is that there are many barriers—both real and imagined—to utilizing health care services.

"Some of these barriers are institutional. Clinical facilities are too far away; they are not open at the time when migrants come in; it takes too long to get an appointment; waiting times within the clinic are lengthy; and the family may move before an office visit can be scheduled," Ryder says. Sometimes the problems are of a personal nature; migrants may be reluctant to seek services because they do not want to bother the doctor over something that might be minor, or they are afraid of what the doctor might find. Other important barriers are related to work and income; migrants cannot always pay for medical care, or cannot afford to lose wages during the time off needed to go see a health care provider.

For the Martinez family, the major obstacles are most of those listed above. Adult migrants often use home remedies or live with the pain until it is unbearable, before seeking medical assistance. However, when children get sick, they are an exception. In fact, medical providers in the Northwest say they are overwhelmed by the large number of children brought by mothers to clinics when migrant families arrive in the area.

A main reason for this is that migrant workers wait until they travel north before seeking medical attention. While still in Texas, Maria Elena had considered seeing a doctor. She needed a tooth pulled, and there were times when she suffered from muscle pains in her left shoulder. But instead of visiting a local health clinic, she said, "I'll wait until we go back to Washington." However, Maria Elena's bad tooth fell out before they left Texas, so no dental visit was needed. As for her muscle pains, she still hasn't seen a doctor. While in Texas, other women who visited the Martinezes talked about taking their children to a physician for common aches and pains, but their response regarding their own ailments was typically, "I'll wait until I go back up north."

There are low-income health clinics available in Texas, and many farm workers' families there do receive medical coupons. But their main reason for waiting until they return "up north" is not based on financial need; rather, they feel more comfortable in the north.

"We've never really gone to the doctor in Texas before," Maria Elena says. "There's never been a serious illness. And we can always wait until we go up north to see the doctor. With the children, we take them for their physicals during the summer, and we're always traveling during that time. So we take them to see a doctor wherever we are." She claims that the doctors she and her family have seen in Washington and Oregon give thorough checkups, while "the doctors back home don't care for the people."

Since male migrant workers rarely step into a health clinic, La Clinica Migrant Health Center in Pasco and the Benton-Franklin Health Department have decided to take their services into the fields. With a $120,000 federal grant awarded in 1991, the two health providers have been able to perform outreach services in rural areas in a program called the Heart Health Project. Recently, the clinic and the health department have provided cholesterol testing and cardiovascular screenings. Testings are planned for every six months, with the first conducted from September to December 1991. During that time, 235 Hispanic migrant workers were observed—135 women and 100 men. "Our findings have indicated that the Hispanic population is not any worse off than the rest of the general population," says Irene Berger, Heart Health Project program director.

According to statistics for people aged 30 to 69 in the "Textbook of Family Practice," one-third of the population of the United States is more than 20 percent overweight. The book also reports that among blacks, 38 percent suffer from high blood pressure, while the figure is 18 percent for whites.

In regard to migrant workers, those aged 30 to 49 are watched most closely for cardiovascular problems, and the testing results have broken down as follows:

- In the 30-39 age group: 14 percent of females and 11 percent of males have high cholesterol levels.
- In the 40-49 age group: 18 percent of females and 9 percent of the males tested with high levels.

According to blood pressure screening results:

- In the 30-39 age group: 11 percent of the women and 17 percent of the men have high blood pressure.
- In the 40-49 age group: high blood pressure in women is 15 percent, while the incidence in men is 14 percent.

Migrant workers also were weighed, indicating:

- 23 percent of the females in the 30-39 age group are overweight, as opposed to only 9 percent of the men.
- In the 40-49 age group, 19 percent of the women are overweight, compared to only 6 percent of the men.

"Women were higher in everything than men, and I would attribute that to the fact that women are more sedate than the men," Berger says. "The women are the ones that stay at home to have children and take care of those they've already had, while the men are getting exercise while working out in the fields." Berger also speculates that many of the women who had worked in the fields also often adopted a sedate lifestyle by about the age of 40, because the difficulties of field labor had forced them to quit working. But, she says, "I expected to find a higher number of at-risk cases because of the diet, which includes a lot of fried foods. But I didn't. I was surprised to find that the numbers were low."

Coordinators say the project has proven beneficial because they have received a high degree of response from the migrant workers. "Everyone is real interested in having their blood and cholesterol levels checked. And when they find that they are at-risk, they're real quick to ask questions of what they can do to improve their health," says Nancy Delgado, outreach worker at La Clinica.

Farm owners in the area also are receptive to having health workers visit farm laborers in the fields and are amenable to setting up times when testing can be conducted. Recently, 16 migrant workers employed at Hogue Farms in Prosser were screened, a process that took two hours.

"We tell the farmers that it's real important that they let us go out into the fields, because otherwise the workers won't come to us," Delgado says. "They don't have time, and certainly won't take time out of work to visit the clinic."

After a test is conducted, another is planned six months later. "This is when we reach the hard part, and when we run into snags, because we try to seek out those that were previously tested and reported to be at-risk to give them a follow-up," Berger says. "And many times they are no longer in the area."

It is also hard to determine if migrant workers are seeking medical attention once they move to a new location. "Follow-ups are very hard, and we can only hope that they do see a physician when needed. But we have no way of knowing," Berger points out. "But the good thing of going back out into the fields six months later is that we have a whole new group of people to test and educate about proper health care."

In contrast to the Pasco and Benton/Franklin county medical services, Walla Walla's Family Medical Center does not provide for medical screening in the fields, but it does accommodate migrants by staying open until 7 p.m. on Thursdays. JoAnn McKern, administrative coordinator, also points out that a few years ago a mobile medical unit traveled to Dayton once a week to provide medical care to field workers there. But that service is no longer available. "And of course our social workers do a lot of in-home visits, and we also provide transportation to migrant workers who need medical assistance and have no way of getting to the clinic," McKern notes.

Medical Care Improvements

In the late 1960s and early 1970s, health workers throughout the country became aware that medical care for migrant workers was almost nonexistent. And, where medical care was sought, it was found that records for migrant workers were rarely kept.

In 1975, the National Migrant Resource Program was formed to track individual migrant workers as they traveled throughout the country. "Our job was to provide health centers along the migrant stream with medical information about these individual workers," explains Roberta Ryder, executive director. "We facilitate the exchange of medical information among community-based migrant health centers in order to achieve continuity of health care for migrant farm workers nationwide."

Since its doors first opened, NMRP has developed a multi-faceted program, offering products and services in support of migrant health facilities. NMRP operates as a referral agency, and provides publications, research, seminars, and workshops for health care workers who deal with migrants. "We serve as a bridge between organizations that are interested in serving migrants, but don't know where to start," Ryder says. "For example, with migrant workers we're talking about people who are usually monolingual and have strong religious or cultural beliefs. Therefore, people who work with them need to understand this. So we offer seminars, publications, and a list of other people and agencies who can help them deal with migrant workers on a one-to-one basis."

One of the major programs operated by the NMRP is the Migrant Clinicians Network, an organization of health and human service professionals who work with migrant and seasonal farm workers. The Clinicians Network was established in 1984 to identify and address clinical issues affecting the health status of farm workers: "There are about 400 health centers in 41 states and Puerto Rico representing a wide range of professional disciplines and areas of expertise, including maternal and child health, dentistry, nursing, mental health, nutrition, gynecology, family medicine, pediatrics, occupational medicine, public health, clinical administration, and research," says Ryder. "It is estimated that these clinics serve about 500,000 migrants each year."

In Washington, five centers operate under the Migrant Clinicians Network; included among these are La Clinica Migrant Health Center in Pasco and the Yakima Valley Farm Workers Clinic, Inc. in Toppenish. Satellite clinics include the Family Medical Center in Walla Walla, the Hermiston Community Health Clinic, and the Milton-Freewater Medical Center. Four centers are located in Oregon at Hood River, Phoenix, Woodburn, and Cornelius.

In Texas, there are 14 centers, with four located in the Rio Grande Valley – Rio Grande City, Pharr, Harlingen, and Brownsville – where a large concentration of migrants live. The facilities are funded by the Migrant Health Program, Bureau of Health Care Delivery and Assistance, Public Health Service, and the U.S. Department of Health and Human Services. "Funding for 1991 was $51.3 million. This money is distributed based on need of each center," Ryder says.

But even with this funding, Ryder believes the amount is not sufficient to provide adequate medical care for migrant workers: "If we do serve 500,000 migrants a year then that is about $100 per individual, per year. The average cost for one doctor's visit is about $30; therefore, an individual may visit a doctor about three times a year. What all this means is that only the most basic care is being provided for migrants. They can go to the doctor for common aches and pain, but should they develop a serious illness or need an operation, where's the money going to come from?"

Ryder claims it is a "crying shame" that not enough federal funding is put into taking care of medical needs of migrant workers. "This is a population at risk, and medical assistance is the last care they seek because they don't have any money."

In the 16 years since the NMRP began operating, Ryder has seen little improvement: "It is difficult to provide change in the population as a whole. We have seen changes in lives of one family, or in curing a serious illness of an individual, or of even getting one family out of the migrant cycle. A lot of good has been done with individuals, but as a whole, nothing has changed. Thirty years ago we had a certain group of migrant workers, today it's another group, and in time there will be another similar group."

She believes that change requires public awareness. "Consumers need to be aware of the role of the worker who is putting food on their table, then they have the power to do something about it." Ryder adds: "There should be a national campaign as there was some years ago when consumers were standing up against the killing of dolphins in the tuna catch. But as long as we keep capitalizing on cheap labor as a source of getting our food, then I don't see an end."

Top ten major and minor illnesses experienced by migrant workers in the U.S. according to the National Migrant Resource Program.

Minor illnesses	Major illnesses
1. Colds	1. Eye problems
2. Headaches	2. Depression
3. Flu	3. Anemia
4. Toothaches	4. Arthritis
5. Ear problems	5. High blood pressure
6 Sore throats	6. Still births
7. Backaches	7. Kidney problems
8. Eye problems	8. Obesity
9. Coughing	9. Pregnancy problems
10. Allergies	10. Asthma

Migrant Malnutrition

Ironically, although migrant workers put fruit and vegetables on America's tables, many infrequently include such produce in their own diets. According to a 1990 study by the Public Voice for Food and Health Policy, of Washington, D. C., migrants remain among the most poorly nourished group of people in the United States. The study was funded by the Rural Economic Policy Program at the Aspen Institute, and the Rural Poverty and Resources Program at the Ford Foundation. Public

Voice for Food and Health Policy is a national research, educational, and advocacy organization that promotes consumer interest in public and private decision-making on food and health issues. The study found that Hispanic migrants' diets are deficient in vitamin A, iron, calcium, and, to a lesser extent, vitamin C. The biggest reason for this malnutrition is poverty.

To some extent, according to the study, the diet of Hispanic migrants is only slightly better than their African-American counterparts. Workers of Haitian descent, who also were included in the study, fared the best in terms of nutrition among the three migrant groups. Dietary inadequacies are most common among migrant females, who are consistently less likely than males to eat food that meets the Recommended Dietary Allowance set by the U.S. Department of Agriculture.

The study listed the following as typical meals for Hispanic migrants:

- Breakfast—Instant coffee with sugar and milk, and pinto beans either boiled with onions or refried in lard or vegetable shortening and served with homemade flour tortillas. Or, fried eggs served with homemade salsa, tortillas, refried beans, and, sometimes, chorizo (sausage) or bacon. Cola drinks are commonly consumed at breakfast.
- Lunch—Tacos made with corn or wheat tortillas and filled with pinto beans, onions, tomatoes, and, sometimes, American cheese. Or, chicken or beef stew, usually including onions, jalapeno peppers, and tomatoes, served with flour tortillas. Reheated beans are sometimes served as well. Lunch drinks usually are Kool-Aid or soft drinks.
- Dinner—Stew made with chicken or beef, rice, tomatoes, and other vegetables, and served with flour tortillas, soft drinks, or Kool-Aid. Or, refried beans with fried eggs, salsa, tomatoes, flour tortillas, and soda or Kool-Aid. Or, a ham sandwich on white bread and soda. Beer, especially among men, and coffee are favorite drinks later in the evening.

While the diet is filling, it is low in nutritional value. "This diet appears to be high in fat and salt, much of which is added to the refried beans, egg dishes, and stews, and low in fruits and fruit juices," Jeff Shotland, director of nutrition of Public Voice for Food and Health Policy, says in a phone interview.

"The infrequent consumption of milk and other dairy products may point to inadequate intake of calcium. Because chili peppers and tomatoes are regularly consumed, it is unlikely that vitamin C, or to a lesser extent, vitamin A are at risk," he points out. "However, I'd like to note that the diet does appear to be otherwise lacking in good sources of vitamin A." He also said that those surveyed had adequate levels of protein, vitamin B, and iron. However, intestinal parasites in migrant workers rob their bodies of iron.

The study doesn't list lack of education as one of the reasons for poor nutrition, although Shotland says education about diet must improve. Aside from poverty, the study listed the following reasons for inadequate nutrition:

- Lack of transportation makes it difficult for some to obtain food stamps, to go to food banks, or take part in nutritional programs for women, infants, and children.
- Inability to find work during a number of months—usually July, August, December, and January. When unable to find work, they only have enough money to purchase the bare necessities.
- Lack of freezers in farm labor camps to store leftovers and inexpensive frozen food products, such as orange juice concentrate.

Other contributing factors are that refrigerators and stoves are commonly run down and in poor repair; some housing does not provide sanitary areas for food preparation; and storage space typically is either lacking or inadequate. "Some migrants also say that a particularly difficult period for them occurs after arrival in a new area. They often do not have work at first, and by the time they receive their first paycheck, several weeks have passed," Shotland says. "Others say that when they are up north, they frequently run out of money for food by the last week of every month."

An inadequate diet, of course, can result in serious health difficulties. Although widely believed to be a problem limited to the Third World, intestinal parasite infection is extremely prevalent in the migrant population, which decreases overall nutrient absorption.

"This is especially detrimental to the infected individual's iron status," Shotland notes. "Iron deficiency anemia is a particular problem among populations with a high prevalence of parasites. Other effects include acute diarrhea and vomiting, particularly among children. Again, the result is decreased absorption and increased loss of several important nutrients, especially water soluble nutrients such as vitamin C and a full range of B vitamins."

As a result of the study, Shotland has recommendations that need to be implemented to eradicate inadequate diets. They include nutrition education workshops for parents, government-financed sanitation improvements at migrant labor camps, and more participation in the food stamp program and the Women, Infant and Children program. The latter could be accomplished by making these program centers more accessible to the labor camps, providing transportation to the centers, and having the centers open more often. "If we really don't take a good, long look at these problems. . .and provide better medical and financial aid, better housing, transportation, field sanitation, and a list of other improvements, then we may never see an end to migrant problems," Shotland concludes.

The diet in the Martinez household is typical of most Hispanic families. A favorite is flour tortillas, served at breakfast, lunch, and supper. Raul does not consider his meal complete unless Maria Elena has cooked a fresh batch of tortillas for him. Every morning, Maria Elena flattens out the flour tortillas with a rolling pin. Most of the time, she prepares the dough the night before: "My family loves tortillas, and they have to eat them with every meal. They rarely eat bread." Refried beans are included in every meal, and it is common for the children to eat tacos made with flour tortillas and refried beans before school and sometimes as a snack in the afternoons. Rice is also frequently eaten, and most evenings Maria Elena will make a stew of ground beef and potatoes.

The typical diet is primarily the result of Hispanic tradition, coupled with poverty. Although the Martinez children enjoy green vegetables and fruits, such as apples, oranges, and grapes, they are rarely purchased at grocery stores because they are too expensive. Family members, however, usually have fresh produce to eat when they are picking such crops as apples, which are given to them free by farmers. Raul and Maria Elena drink coffee during breakfast, lunch, and dinner, while the children drink milk most of the time, although they sometimes will have Kool-Aid and, rarely, soft drinks.

An important thing I have noticed about the diet of the Martinezes, and most migrant workers, is that "junk food" is seldom found in the house. Potato chips, candy, and cookies are seldom purchased because they cost too much. When surviving on a limited income, only the necessities are bought.

Chapter 6

Job Hazards

For years, agriculture has been recognized as one of the nation's most hazardous industries, and one of the biggest concerns attracting public attention has been the effects of pesticides on farm workers. As a result, the U.S. Environmental Protection Agency has established regulations to insure that proper steps are taken to protect field workers.

In the state of Washington, the Department of Labor and Industries monitors compliance with the regulations; in 1991, the agency received 117 complaints filed against farm owners. Fifty percent of these complaints occurred in orchard work, 22 percent on other types of farms, and the remaining 28 percent in greenhouses and from crop dusting. Susan Taylor, public information officer with the Department of Labor and Industries in Olympia, reports that 49 complaints came from Yakima County, 10 from Benton County, 9 from Franklin County, and 2 from Walla Walla County. In all, 76 percent of all claims were from Eastern Washington. "Of course, we understand that a lot of claims go unreported," she says.

Taylor notes that 42 percent of the claims reported in 1991 dealt with direct exposure from spraying and other application of pesticides while workers were in the fields, or from the mixing of pesticide chemicals. Twenty-one percent concerned pesticide drift or chemical residue on fruits.

When a complaint is filed, Labor and Industries sends out a safety inspector to investigate the claim. "If the complaint regards danger to life or health, then we take action within 24 hours," comments Ismael Rodriguez, safety inspector in Kennewick. "If there is cause for danger, then we have up to three days for action. And for other complaints, we have 20 days to move in."

If immediate action is needed, an inspector enters the fields and stops all activity. "Workers are told to leave the fields," Rodriguez says. "The farmer is fined, and that amount depends on the severity of what we have found, and the farmer's reaction." Although he has never had a problem with farmers ignoring directives that workers leave fields to avoid pesticide exposure, Rodriguez said other inspectors have.

There are three ways that poisons can enter the body: pesticide fumes or dust can be inhaled, the skin or other body tissues can absorb chemicals, or pesticides can be swallowed. The most common signs of poisoning are sleepiness, headaches, dizziness, excessive sweating, blurred vision, vomiting, muscle pains, stomach aches, and cramps. A person poisoned by pesticides will normally have three or more of these symptoms occurring soon after exposure or later the same day. Signs of serious poisoning, which can lead to death, include trouble with breathing, drooling, fluid loss from the nose, pupils that won't dilate, and a loss of consciousness.

The Environmental Protection Agency, in an agreement with the U.S. Department of Agriculture Extension Service, has published a booklet entitled "Pesticide Safety for Farmworkers." This booklet, written in English and Spanish, lists precautions that should be taken by field workers to avoid and treat pesticide poisoning. Although some of the precautions listed may be considered common sense, EPA officials say they feel the booklet is necessary because some farm workers may not know how to protect themselves. While in the fields, pesticide poisoning can be stopped by rinsing chemicals off skin and clothing with water from a lake, field tank, or irrigation ditch. As soon as possible, a shower must be taken with soap and water, and the hair shampooed. Contaminated clothes must be washed before being worn again.

Some pesticides can cause rashes or burn the skin, resulting in redness, itchiness, and water blisters. Redness and soreness of the eyes can result from splashing chemicals, or rubbing the eyes with a sleeve or hand that has pesticides on it. Pesticide residues can remain in fields for up to two weeks, and they cannot always be seen, so field workers need to cover up as much skin as possible. Common work clothes should include long-sleeve shirts, long pants, hats, socks, shoes or boots, and gloves that can be thoroughly cleaned.

Field workers are also informed about safe pesticide use practices. These include washing hands and face before eating, drinking, smoking, or going to the bathroom. Fruits and vegetables taken directly from the field must be washed before eating. Work clothes should be washed separately from other laundry, and hands and arms must be washed after putting work clothes into a washing machine.

After spraying, sufficient time must pass before laborers can safely enter a field, and the EPA booklet emphasizes to workers that they must not enter in violation of warning signs, even if farmers ask or tell them to do so. This waiting time is called the re-entry period. Furthermore, workers should be given a written notice or verbal warning not to go into a field without special protective clothing until the re-entry period is up. "These rules should be told or handed out to workers by the farmer before they are to start a new job and it should be stated in the language that the worker is familiar with," Rodriguez says.

Members of the Martinez family have suffered from headaches, red eyes, and nausea because of spraying or other forms of pesticide application. "I remember there were times when headaches were so bad, we would just collapse when we got home," Maria Elena recalls.

"We try to take care of ourselves. We at least make sure we wear proper clothing, and I know better than to go into a field that has been sprayed," Raul says. "My job is important. But my health is more important because without it, I wouldn't be able to do my work."

The Martinezes talk about field workers they have known who have suffered from skin blisters, and children being born with deformities—they believe this is due to mothers working in fields when pesticides were applied. "Most of these people don't go to the doctor when they get sick; instead, they just take care of themselves at home," Maria Elena says. "Most of the time they don't go to the doctor because they can't afford to."

Raul explains that some workers who suffer pesticide poisoning do so because they choose not to leave fields during spraying, they ignore warning signs and enter fields soon after spraying, or they do not take proper precautions such as wearing the right kind of clothing. "And other times it's that the farmer just doesn't care and doesn't give warning after a field has been sprayed." However, Raul has not had any problems with farmers for whom he has worked.

"If we hear of problems or if we encounter problems, it is not with our farmer, but with another one," he says. "For example, when our farmers spray pesticides, they tell us—and we can't enter the fields again until it's safe. The problem is that when we're working our fields, another farmer may be spraying his field which is next to ours, and we get all the drifting. That's when we begin to suffer from headaches or red and itchy eyes."

Raul makes sure all precautions are taken so he and his family do not suffer from pesticide poisoning. Proper clothes are worn, and their food is not carried with them into the fields. Showers are taken immediately once they return home, and all produce brought directly from the fields is thoroughly washed. "We've never suffered from anything major. And as for the headaches or red eyes, I just wait for it to go away."

A 1988 survey conducted by Evergreen Legal Services found that less than 15 percent of farm workers in Washington who experience ill effects from pesticides seek medical treatment. The survey said farm workers are unaware that their medical bills would be covered by workers' compensation. Furthermore, workers may fear employer disapproval if it is discovered they have reported that their illness was caused by unsafe farming practices.

Other Injuries in the Fields

In addition to pesticide-use problems, field workers can also file claims for job-related injuries with the Washington State Department of Labor and Industries. The agency reports that some 23,880 workers' compensation claims were filed by farm workers between 1987 and 1990. Yakima County accounted for most, or 30 percent, of those claims. Other counties in the top 10 were Benton County, fifth in the list with 6 percent of the claims; and Franklin County, sixth with 5 percent of all claims. Walla Walla County did not make the top 10.

Sprains were the most common type of injury cited on farm worker claims during the three-year period. Cuts, dizziness, scratches, fractures, ill-defined symptoms, and multiple injuries were the next most common medical problems. Thirty claimants were 12 years of age or younger, but the majority were in their 20s.

The most common farming fatalities, or 26 percent, are caused by tractor rollovers. In fact, fatalities frequently are machinery related. "Working in the fields or in a storage shed is a dangerous job, and sometimes the farmer or crew leader does not take the time to go over safety rules and regulations with the workers," says Fedencia Barrera, a migrant worker and friend of the Martinez family. "So it's up to us to look after each other and to teach each other how to use the machines properly. When we work in the hops and are working with machines, I've had to tell people to wear their clothes, shirt tails, and long-sleeves, tucked in, tie their hair back, and to make sure their shoelaces are properly tied," Barrera says. "Once those machines get going, they're real powerful and it's very easy to get caught in one and lose an arm or leg."

In the past, members of the Martinez family have received cuts and scratches from knives and scissors when cutting asparagus and onions.

"Bruises and cuts I can handle, that's why I never go see a doctor," Raul says. "But I think if I suffered a major illness from the pesticides then I would go see a doctor because pesticide poisoning is not something to be taken lightly."

Farm Worker Safety: New Regulations

In the past two decades, farmers in Washington and Oregon have been inundated with rules and regulations regarding farm work safety. Rules cover everything from field sanitation and living conditions in labor camps, to hazard communication and occupational safety. Most of these rules were passed in the mid-1970s and have been revised by the Washington and Oregon state legislators following further, extensive study and research.

Two farmers who were willing to speak with the *Walla Walla Union-Bulletin* said that although the intent of the laws is good, they require a lot of paperwork. "These laws force the farmers to sit up and pay attention, so it's only natural that there is going to be some resistance," points out Dave LeFore, a farmer from Milton-Freewater.

"The concept is good because it provides for a safe and healthy atmosphere for farm workers. Insurance rates for farm work are very high and that reflects that these types of jobs can be hazardous," he says. "But the only problem I see is that farm work is not organized like factories and yet we're expected to operate like big businesses." For about the past 10 years, LeFore has maintained a beekeeping operation, and 50 acres of apple and plum orchards. LeFore employs 6 year-round farm workers, and about 12 seasonal laborers.

Another farmer, Kent Waliser, also of Milton-Freewater, emphasizes that state and federal agencies keep requiring more paperwork from farmers as years go by. "The intent of all this is to provide a safer, healthier workplace for the employee, but what it's done is increase the cost of doing business," Waliser says. "The agriculture business has had to adopt some of the safety requirements that are used in big industries, and some of these farmers have not been used to this before."

One example is the creation of safety committees. In March 1991, the Oregon Legislature passed a law requiring that prior to commencing work, employers must hold safety meetings at the job site. These meetings must allow a question-and-answer period with the foreman or man in charge. At the meetings, safety and health issues are discussed, and workers are informed of their right to report workplace hazards and are encouraged to make such reports. "We are forced into formal changes that we're not used to, and that can cause a burden on the farmers," LeFore notes.

But, as some farmers are quick to point out, most of these rules and regulations are needed for the safety and health of the workers. An example of this are provisions regarding field sanitation, which require potable drinking water, and toilet and handwashing facilities. The laws in both states are the same: they require that drinking water be provided and placed in locations readily accessible to all employees; that containers be refilled daily or more often if necessary; that water be dispensed in single-use drinking cups or by angle jet fountains; that common drinking cups or dippers be prohibited; and that water be suitably cool at 60 degrees or less. During hot weather, a thirsty worker may require up to three gallons of water per day.

Another health requirement for agriculture workers became effective in 1988 in Oregon, and a short time later in Washington as well. This law requires that one toilet facility be provided for each 20 employees; that toilets be inspected at the start of each day and supplied with toilet paper; and that they be adequately ventilated, appropriately screened, have self-closing doors that can be closed and latched from the inside, and constructed as to ensure privacy. Also, employees must be allowed reasonable opportunities during the work period to use the facilities.

"State legislatures have worked real hard to try to protect the rights of farm workers and to provide them safe conditions to work under," says Tomas Schwabe, agricultural health supervisor with the Oregon Occupational Safety and Health Act office in Salem. "The level of compliance in field sanitation has improved significantly, but we still have a number of non-compliance employers which OSHA is specifically targeting for action."

Regarding field sanitation, there were 3.5 violations per inspection in 1985, says Schwabe. In 1986, that number dropped to 2.6. However, violations crept back up to 3.2 in 1987, and to 3.3 in 1988. A year later, the number dropped to 1.8.

"In general, farmers show that they're willing to comply, but like any rules, there are some that don't agree with some of the rules," says Paul Merrill, senior safety inspector with Washington's Department of Labor and Industries, Division of Industrial Safety and Health. "We have had some problems here and there in the past couple of years, but we've gotten it cleaned up. Most are very cooperative and they show a lot of common sense."

But there are some farmers who are hostile about the strict enforcements. "All of these rules are new to the agriculture industry and to the migrants themselves. I mean we're dealing with people who come from a society and culture where there are no rules and whose education level is well below the Caucasian. So, aside from following rules, the farmer has to do a lot of educating," Waliser says. "I suppose a lot of people see it as a real burden, and it has been."

In both states, penalties are strict if a farmer is found in violation. "Penalties can run anywhere from $50 to $7,000 per violation," Schwabe points out. "But in general, we're seeing that farmers are complying. I know it hasn't been easy for them, because there are pages and pages of rules and regulations. But they are needed and they protect the employee as well as the employer."

Chapter 7

The Journey Home

SINCE EARLY SEPTEMBER, migrant families have been leaving the Northwest, returning home to Texas or Mexico. Trucks loaded with personal belongings and packed to capacity with people can be spotted passing through nearby Hermiston, Umatilla, and Irrigon. Maria Elena finds herself stopping to ask families where they are coming from and where they are heading. Most are from western Washington on their way to Texas. They say that strawberry and raspberry harvests west of the Cascades have been ruined by severe rain. Instead of traveling to other parts of the country to find work, they have decided to go home and wait until spring to return.

For the migrant families in Boardman, however, work has been available. Most migrants here are employed in the potato harvest, which is not expected to be completed until late autumn. Of the families in the Boardman area, however, the Martinezes will be among the first to leave for Texas.

"I've been wanting to leave since September, but then Raul went and got that job picking apples," Maria Elena says almost bitterly.

"Well, last year we left in early October and then we found ourselves bored in Texas without any money coming in," her husband responds. "So this year I decided to stay here as long as we can, and if we can earn more money, that's even better for us." To go with the $4,000 Raul earned cutting asparagus, he has added about $1,000 for hoeing onion, potato, and tomato crops, and about $2,000 for picking apples.

"This wasn't a very good year for us in the fields," Maria Elena says. "Last year we earned about $8,000 for the year and I think this year we'll only make $6,000. I think we only have about $1,400 left for the road and to carry us through next spring plus what we'll get from welfare."

In trying to give Raul a little push to decide to head home soon, about two weeks ago Maria Elena began putting up pictures of family members throughout the apartment. Included are photos of the two new grandsons in Texas. The fact that Raul has been able to obtain employment through October is one reason why the family hasn't left sooner, but another factor is that he has been waiting for the time when other families will leave, so they can travel south together in a convoy. The eldest of the Martinez children, Raul, Jr., and his wife and daughter, are expected to leave Boardman later in the fall after the potato harvest, and so are other friends and relatives.

"I don't like for my sons to travel home alone because so many things have happened on the road," Raul says. "When there are a lot of families traveling together, at least there are people to help each other out if something happens."

The late autumn trip might be hard and long for Raul and Maria Elena, so they have decided to send for a son-in-law in Texas to meet them here and help with the driving. Their son-in-law, Christobal Saenz, will be arriving by plane. Saenz is a migrant crew leader, who this year brought workers to asparagus fields in Othello, and needs to speak with the owner regarding plans for next spring's harvest.

"He had to come up here and speak with the farmer anyway, so he wanted to wait until we were ready to leave so he could arrange to come up here and help us with the driving back home," Maria Elena says. "It's hard for just Raul by himself, because I don't know how to drive and, of course, Jimmy and Billy can't help."

As the days get closer for the family to leave, all eyes and ears are on the weather forecast. Maria Elena keeps talking about seeing her other children. Jimmy keeps mentioning playing with his friends when he gets home, and Billy asks every morning, "Is today our last day here?"

I've been wondering the same thing, and riding an emotional roller coaster for the past two weeks since Maria Elena first informed me that we would be leaving the area and returning to Texas any day now. One day it's, "We're leaving tomorrow," and the next day it's, "No, we're leaving next week." For me, I'm sitting one day in my friend's living room, crying and preparing myself to say good-bye to all the wonderful people I've come to know here, and the next day I'm telling her, "We're staying here one more week. So, ready to party again this weekend?"

I go into Walla Walla every weekend to gain some distance and regain perspective. I have to keep reminding myself that I am a reporter living with this family to get an inside view of how they live, and it is important to keep that separation and not get too engulfed in the family. Going to Walla Walla has helped me do that, but I've also settled into a routine. I've been able to meet new people, socialize with friends, and maintain some of my independent, single life that I don't have when I'm with the Martinez family. But the hard part is that I've become attached to some people, therefore saying good-bye is not something I look forward to.

To a certain extent, I've had to start thinking as a migrant does. I meet someone, I get to know them and enjoy their company, but in the back of my head I must remember that any day now I will be packing my things to move more than 2,000 miles away.

I asked Maria Elena how she can handle this daily, emotional turmoil: "That's just the way we are and the way we've always been. We never know what's going to happen from one day to the next because plans change so much. Even when we're preparing to come up here, our plans change daily. It's just something you get used to."

Although the constant relocating and resettling may come easy for Raul and Maria Elena, it hasn't been easy for their children. In early September, when Jimmy and Billy were enrolled in school here, Jimmy was very eager to go to school every day and see his friends. But as the month went by, I started noticing a change in him. Then one day he asked me, "It's sad when you have to say good-bye to your friends, isn't it?" Not knowing what he was getting at, I pursued his questioning even further. He finally told me that although he has a lot of friends in school, he doesn't like to get too close to them because he knows he's going to have to say good-bye.

"The same thing happened when we were in Pasco. I made a lot of friends there, but then we left and I don't think I'll see them again. And now the same thing is going to happen here. It's sad, I don't like to say good-bye," Jimmy says.

Charlie also purposely avoided establishing any type of relationship with people. He told me once a few months ago that he considered himself to be alone. The few friends he did have came from other migrant families. "At least, if they're migrant workers I know I will see them when we're traveling around," Charlie says.

Thinking back on this, I've come to understand why migrant families are a very close group and why they are so family-oriented. They are all they have. They rely on one another for moral, emotional, and financial support, and in many instances will travel together throughout the country looking for work. And it is very common for migrant families to intermarry.

Although it's time for me to say good-bye to people here whom I've spent time with and have gotten to know, admire, like, and respect, I know it's not forever. I will be back. I've prepared myself emotionally for this. But for kids to purposely avoid seeking friends and establishing any type of bond with other people at such a young age, life must be very, very lonely.

On the Road

It is 9 a.m. Monday, October 28, and the Martinez family is leaving Boardman, Oregon, to return to South Texas for the winter. At 6 a.m., the Martinezes and two other families start loading cars and trucks with their personal belongings. They have checked and rechecked the vehicles, making sure they are in good working condition, and saying good-bye to friends they have made while living in Boardman.

The first stop is 17 miles down the road in Hermiston, where they spend four hours taking care of last-minute business. Checks have to be cashed, unemployment benefit forms have to be filed, and groceries bought. Finally, at 1 p.m., a caravan of two trucks and two cars heads out on the long trek south. The vehicles are filled to capacity with boxes, green garbage bags, grocery bags, and clothes that are folded and placed wherever there is room. All 13 people – eight adults and five children – are excited. Their enthusiasm grows as they come upon the snow-covered evergreens lining Interstate 84 near La Grande, Oregon.

Raul and Maria Elena are in the lead truck with Billy, who sits in his mother's lap. Christobal Saenz, the Martinezes' son-in-law, is at the wheel. Following close behind is another car in which Jimmy is a passenger. Behind that car is a friend of the Martinez family, Alejandro Martinez, 32; his wife, Angelica, 24; and their 5- and 15-month-old daughters. In the rear is Raul Martinez Jr., his wife, Iris, and their 4-year-old daughter, Abby. Christobal and Raul Jr. – because they were the most experienced on the road – will often lead the caravan or bring up the rear during the four-day, 2,141-mile trip.

Upon entering Idaho, the caravan stops at the first rest area, near Caldwell. The women head for a telephone to call their families in Texas, while the men check the vehicles. The kids run to the bathroom. After a few minutes, everyone is back in the vehicles and the traveling continues. As night falls, the weather gets colder.

At about 1 a.m., Tuesday, the caravan reaches Salt Lake City, where signs of winter can be seen. Snow lines the highways and snow flurries fall. The caravan stays together, each driver following as close as possible to avoid getting lost. After driving 645 miles in 12 hours, we pull in late at a Motel 6 in Provo and settle in. After a brief night's sleep, 5:30 a.m. wake-up calls come. "It seems like we just went to sleep," Iris says. "What time did we get here?" she asks.

"1:30 a.m." Maria Elena replies.

"No. 2:30 a.m. We're now on Mountain time, not Pacific time. We lost an hour of sleep," Alejandro says.

Moaning and groaning is heard. Yet everyone crawls into their vehicles without saying a word. The difficult driving now begins. A snowstorm hits as the caravan approaches a canyon near Utah Lake. Vehicles became separated, but drivers know to continue on until they get out of the canyon. It is two hours of tension—and slow, careful driving along the winding roads overlooking steep cliffs. The sky is gray and snow keeps falling rapidly. Snowplows pass to clear the roads. No one speaks. Ahead, an overturned truck and trailer can be seen. Hearts start beating faster as an ambulance arrives; the travelers in the caravan pray.

After two hours of what seems like endless driving, the last car in the caravan clears the canyon, and all four vehicles stop at a gas station. Everyone's knees are trembling when getting out of the cars and trucks. As the men check the vehicles and tires, the women quietly walk into the gas station to buy coffee. The kids talk about how scary it was.

"I remember when Jimmy was only 41 days old and we came through that canyon. I was holding him so tight," Maria Elena recalls. "And to top it off, one of the windows of the truck was broken, so all this snow kept coming in. We were all frozen of cold and fright."

"Once when I was little my family came through there at night and the road was closed," Iris adds. "We had to spend the night in the canyon. I remember my father had to keep turning on the engine and putting on the heater so we wouldn't freeze."

Recovering from fright, the kids begin playing in the snow. Someone turns on a portable radio, and the announcer says that the road through the canyon has just been closed. Everyone looks at each other nervously, and without a word they climb back into the vehicles and drive off. Ahead lay another dangerous section of highway near Arches National Park in Utah. Luckily, conditions there turn out to be nothing compared to what we have just passed through — only light snow is encountered. But engine problems keep forcing Raul to pull over to the shoulder.

Finally, reaching Moab, Utah, we pull into a McDonald's. Raul Jr. checks his father's truck. Realizing there is a problem with the carburetor, he sets out to buy a part. "The truck kept rattling and shaking so bad. I didn't think we were going to make it," Maria Elena comments.

The rest of the day is filled with more snow, rain, clouds, and cold weather. After 13 hours and 590 miles, we reach Albuquerque and settle in at a Motel 6 for another night of sleep.

By 7 a.m., Wednesday, it is back on the road again. Albuquerque is sunny, but 45-mph gusts of wind and 35-degree weather make it unbearable to be outdoors. Alejandro Martinez and his family decide to take off ahead. "We really want to get home today. We don't have any more money in case everyone wants to spend one more night somewhere," Alejandro says.

"That was a bad move on their part. They should have waited for all of us to leave together," Raul Jr. later says.

"If they don't have any money, any one of us would be happy to lend them some," adds Iris.

"I'm worried about those babies. What if something happens on the road and they don't have any money?" Maria Elena asks.

The three remaining families are greeted with sleet and freezing temperatures an hour after leaving Albuquerque. From there to Roswell, New Mexico, the vehicles have to pull over about every 30 minutes to scrape ice off the windshields.

About 30 minutes after lunch, the caravan enters Texas, and everyone gives a sigh of relief. But it will take another day of traveling before reaching their home in LaGrulla, so the families decide to spend the night in Del Rio. We traveled 602 miles in 15 hours on this third day.

Thursday, October 31, everyone awakes at 6 a.m. Outside in the parking lot, the kids excitedly run around, talking about getting home and what they are going to wear for Halloween. The day is cloudy and rainy, but temperatures are in the 50s. The caravan speeds up to 70-75 mph. There is another 304 miles to go.

In Laredo, everyone stops to refuel and call their families. "We'll be home in about two hours," Maria Elena tells one of her daughters. As she hangs up the phone, she says, "They're waiting for us with a big homecoming dinner."

At the Wheel

And I, for one, was more than relieved to be "home." I'm not one to travel long distances for a long period of time. Whenever I need to get to a certain destination I travel by plane. It's fast and easy. But in order to do my job properly, I had to travel the 2,141 miles from Oregon to South Texas with the Martinez and other migrant families. To put it in a few words, it wasn't fun.

The first day was all right. I guess the excitement and newness kept me going. But that wore off real fast. What really got to me – and quite honestly, got me terrified – was driving through the snowstorm in Utah. I've never driven through that type of weather before, much less through a canyon. I'm from San Antonio, Texas, where we may get one inch of snow every 10 years. I had had three hours of sleep after driving 13 hours the day before and then I found myself under horrible weather conditions. It took about two hours to drive through the canyon near Utah Lake. I also happened to be the last car in our caravan. All I kept repeating to myself was, "You can't stop now. Just keep driving and continue on ahead." I also kept hearing one of the last things a friend in Walla Walla said to me the night before I left: "Be careful, drive carefully and take care of yourself. But most importantly, drive carefully."

When we pulled over to regain composure and to make sure everyone was all right, one of the other drivers practically had to pry my hands off the steering wheel. I was also in desperate need of a cigarette. And I don't smoke.

It was at that moment that I stopped and looked around and noticed that I was the only woman driver in our group. There were four men, four women, and five children. The men knew how to drive, as did three of the women. Yet I was the only one who ever got behind the wheel. The other women were always passengers.

After we drove through the snowstorm in Utah and later the next day through sleet and icy-road conditions in New Mexico, the men would good-humoredly joke about me and how scared I was. Raul would even say, "But you were never scared when you would drive by yourself from Boardman to Walla Walla every weekend. And there you drove at night and went 80 mph."

He exaggerated a bit, yet I did point out to him that I always drove in good weather conditions. Only after the men continued joking about me for a while longer did Iris speak up. "That was the first time she ever drove in snow and she did it by herself," she said. "None of us [women] have ever tried it." That kept the men quiet for the rest of the trip.

Maria Elena also kept pointing out to everyone that I drove most of those 2,000 miles without much help. Christobal did take over the wheel of my car twice: when we got out of the snowstorm because I was too nervous to continue, and once at night because I was too sleepy.

The rest of the trip went by without much mishap, although I did go over a deer that was dead on the road, and a skunk. The smell in my car was unbearable for days, but after that snowstorm I felt I could handle anything.

This trip taught me something about myself: that placed under any condition or situation, I don't give up. But what I really wanted to learn was what pushes the migrant workers to such extremes. I didn't learn that, and I don't know if I ever will.

During the preparation for returning to Texas, and while on the road, I learned that they wait until the last minute to do things. And then, they are always in a hurry. We knew on October 23 that we were going to head home five days later. I had been packed for two weeks. When I returned to Boardman from Walla Walla the Sunday night prior to our departure, I found the families still packing their belongings. It was midnight and things were still scattered throughout the apartment. So I asked Iris, "When did you start packing?"

"Today," she answered.

Then I asked Maria Elena, "If you knew for days that we were leaving on Monday, why did you wait until Sunday to start packing?"

"I don't know," she said, almost embarrassed. "Because that's the way we are, I guess."

Then there was the road trip. We spent 12 to 15 hours in the vehicles each day, without much sleep and only stopping once per day for a warm meal. The rest of the time we halted only to refuel and to ask each of the drivers if they could continue another 300 miles or so. I understand our trying to stay ahead of the terrible weather that was heading our way, but there was also their mentality of hurrying to get home. Christobal had even told me, "Once we made it from Texas to Walla Walla in two days." And he was very proud of that.

So I asked him, "If you know that you're supposed to start a certain job with a harvest on a certain date, then why don't you prepare yourselves and give yourselves ample time to get there without having to drive such forsaken hours without sleep?"

He too looked at me embarrassed and only said, "I don't know."

I asked Maria Elena the same thing and reminded her that just four months ago her son, daughter-in-law, and two grandchildren were in a car accident as they were heading home to Texas. Her son had fallen asleep at the wheel and their truck overturned.

Maria Elena just stared at me and said, "I don't know. That's the way all migrants are. But don't ask me why because I don't know."

The Arrival

Fighting back tears and with ear-to-ear smiles, the Martinezes are reunited with their family after seven months of separation. After the truck and car carrying Raul, Maria Elena, Jimmy, and Billy pull up to their home, the children and grandchildren they had left behind greet them with hugs and kisses.

Although the trip has taken its toll on everyone, enthusiasm is running high as they jump out of the vehicles to greet friends and family. The cloudy, rainy weather does not dampen spirits. The scene is typical this time of year in LaGrulla and elsewhere in The Valley, the area of South Texas that is a permanent home to many migrant workers.

The first in the Martinez caravan to arrive was Raul, the two boys, and son-in-law Christobal. About 15 minutes later Maria Elena arrived. Immediately, her sons and daughter Doris ran to the car to meet their mother. In all the excitement, Maria Elena had difficulty unbuckling her seat belt. No words were exchanged between mother and children, only warm embraces and joyful looks through watery eyes.

Raul Jr., Iris, and Abby first stopped to visit with Iris's family. They arrived at the Martinez home an hour later with Iris's family.

Raul and Maria Elena are led to the house. But before they can enter, Maria Elena's mother, Manuela Solis, 78, walks outside to hug her daughter. Again, no words are spoken, and everyone smiles as they give each other a long embrace. Once inside the house, the parents walk around to get reacquainted with their house. Doris and Robert have been living in the home while their parents were in the Pacific Northwest. Charlie joined Doris and Robert in late August.

"Well, the house is clean, but I don't like the curtains in my bedroom," Maria Elena tells her daughter in Spanish. "And we need to put in some brighter light bulbs in some of the rooms." Doris patiently keeps smiling at her mother while repeating, "Yes, mom. Yes, mom."

Outside, the Martinezes' sons begin unloading the family truck.

"The boxes with kitchen stuff stay in the kitchen, the rest of the boxes go in the back rooms until your mother is ready to unload them," Manuela Solis instructs her grandchildren in Spanish. "When my husband and I came home from the harvest we always made sure everything was put in the back rooms. We tried to keep the front rooms clean for company to drop by."

The daughters start unpacking utensils and nonperishables and putting them in the cupboards. After the truck is unloaded, the sons wash it. Billy and Jimmy begin running and playing in the backyard with their cousins, as word spreads quickly in the tiny community of LaGrulla, population 1,445, that the Martinezes have arrived. Almost instantly the house is filled with neighbors and other family members, such as Raul's brothers and his 91-year-old father. The next two hours are filled with hugs and kisses. Everyone enjoys a warm meal of "mole"—a traditional Mexican dish of chicken served with a dark, thick, spicy chili gravy—rice, potato salad, grilled chicken, and sausage.

"Every time we come home, this is how we are greeted. My children spend the entire morning preparing a dish of 'mole,' and they're the ones who unpack and put everything away for me," Maria Elena says as she sits at the table, relaxing while sipping a cup of coffee.

One of her sons brings in a crate of apples that Raul picked while working in Boardman. Almost instantly the Martinez children begin putting the apples in sacks to take home. Raul begins talking to his sons and sons-in-law about this year's apple harvest and the amount of money earned.

As the evening wears on, more family and friends stop by the house to welcome the family back. Doris takes Jimmy and Billy to the bathroom, where she cuts their hair.

"It was too long. I can't believe you let them wear it like that, Mom," Doris tells Maria Elena. Her mother looks at her and replies, "We didn't have money to cut it, and I don't know how to cut hair."

The highlight of the day is seeing the two new additions to the Martinez family—the infants are now 3-months and 6-months old.

Three hours after the family arrives, Charlie walks through the front door. He has been at school. "There he is," Maria Elena exclaims, and runs to hug her son. She had not seen Charlie since August, when he decided to leave Boardman and return to Texas by bus. "You look so good," she keeps repeating to him. Charlie walks slowly, almost shyly, over to his father to shake his hand, then runs out the back door to look for his younger brothers.

The Martinezes are glad to see that all of their family members are in good health. The only tragedy occurring while they were gone was the burglarizing of Raul Jr. and Iris's home in Mission, Texas. Someone had pried open the burglar bars on the windows. Their television set and hunting rifles were the only things taken, but the rest of the house was vandalized. No one was caught, but the house was insured.

"This happened a few weeks ago, when we were in Boardman. That's when we found out," Iris says, sounding disgusted.

"Well, it's all right. As long as we all got here fine and everyone is in good health," Maria Elena says, trying to comfort her daughter-in-law.

"That's true, but still you leave your homes, travel thousands of miles to work real hard to earn some money, just to have someone break into your home to be mean," Iris responds.

It is Halloween. As nighttime approaches, the families begin preparing to go home and get their children ready for trick-or-treating. That night, with painted faces and plastic bags in hand, Billy and Jimmy go knocking on doors with their cousins. Maria Elena stays at home to talk with her mother, Raul spends time next door with his sons. After a day of excitement and exhaustion everyone goes to sleep at 11 p.m.

The next day Raul and Maria Elena prepare to go into "el pueblo," which in English means "the town," but is commonly used here to refer to the community of Rio Grande, located about 13 miles northwest of LaGrulla. The Martinezes will do some grocery shopping and enroll Jimmy and Billy in school.

"This is where we'll be the next four or five months, and we need to get back to normal," Maria Elena says. "It's good to be back home."

The Reception

On the day we arrive in LaGrulla, at about 1 p.m., I meet the entire Martinez family—the other 10 children, 13 grandchildren, aunts, uncles, cousins, grandparents, and all the in-laws. There must be 100 people in the house this day. I feel rather awkward because they all know I am a newspaper reporter living with the family for a year to document their lives. Yet everyone comes up and speaks to me as if I were a member of the family. Raul and Maria Elena introduce me to their other children as "the newest addition," or "their other sister." To the grandchildren, I am introduced as "their newest aunt."

To a certain extent, I feel like I know the rest of the family as well. While we were living in Boardman, from July 22 to October 28, Maria Elena and I spent our days cooking, cleaning, and washing while talking about our families. After four months, I guess it would be easy to know every member of the family by name, although we had never met.

As soon as we arrived, Doris took me to the bedroom designated for me. The sons unloaded and washed my car, and asked me how I was after the long drive. Meanwhile, I tried to take pictures to run in the newspaper.

The most flattering moment and one I'll always remember is when I met Maria Elena's mother, Manuela Solis. She walked out to the backyard to greet her daughter and son-in-law. As she hugged Maria Elena, the rest of the family gathered around in a semicircle, all with smiling faces and laughing. I was in the background, taking pictures. Almost instantly, she stopped, looked at me and said in Spanish, "This is the young lady I want to meet." Silence fell over the crowd. I stopped taking pictures and lowered my camera. She walked over and extended her hand.

"Welcome to the family," Manuela said. We hugged, and with that everyone started talking and laughing again. To be accepted by the matriarch of the family means to be accepted by the rest—and it was at that moment that I realized I was.

Later in the evening, Doris and another daughter, Ellen Herbert, sit down at the table and look me in the eye.

"So how has it been living with my family?" Doris asks. We talk and joke for hours about the past four months. I also find it fascinating that the older Martinez children ask me, and not their parents, how Jimmy and Billy did in school. Ellen also points out that Billy's English had improved dramatically.

"I guess a lot of that is because of school and by having you live with them," she tells me in English. "Mom said you speak nothing but English to the boys."

And then I see Charlie after two months. I was a little wary of seeing him again. When I first moved in with the family in Walla Walla in July, Charlie was the hardest one to get to know. He had built a huge wall between us, and I remember asking friends of mine in Walla Walla what I should do to get him on my side. I even asked his parents. I was always told, "Just give him time." I did. And with a lot of effort on my part and after traveling with him for four days on the bus to Texas in August, we got to be rather good friends. Yet, I still thought that maybe once again that wall would be built and once again I'd have to find a way to tear it down. I am wrong.

When he arrives home from school, the first person he greets is his mother, of course. I am in the bedroom and hear him arrive, so I walk out into the hall only to find him coming to see me.

"Oh, there you are," he says smiling, extending his hand. "How are you? How was the trip?" he asks in English. I tell him he looks great, that his hair is much shorter than I last remembered. Then he went to greet his father and younger brothers.

Later that night and the next day he jokes with me about the long drive, and asks if he could drive my car and if he could accompany me while I went driving around LaGrulla and other surrounding communities to take pictures. Of course, I say yes. There is no wall between us now.

The rest of the evening the Martinez house is filled with shaking hands, embracing people, and putting names and faces together. At about 9 p.m., while we all sit around the table, I ask, "Well, is that it? Have I met everyone I'm supposed to meet?" Laughing, Maria Elena answers, "Yes, that's it." And with that, I excuse myself and go into the bedroom to unpack, allowing Maria Elena to spend some private moments with her daughters and mother without having a newspaper reporter nearby.

Part II
November-February

Chapter 8

The South Texas Valley

A GREAT NUMBER of migrant farm workers who travel annually to the Pacific Northwest are from a section of the Rio Grande country known as the South Texas Valley, situated in the southern tip of Texas. They leave their homes, they say, because there aren't sufficient or well-paying jobs for them in the Valley.

"The Rio Grande Valley is one of the most depressed areas of the country," admits Texas state representative Rene O. Oliveira, D-Brownsville. "And the reasons are because of natural disasters. . .and inadequate responses from Washington."

The South Texas Valley, which the Martinezes call their home, consists of Willacy, Cameron, Hidalgo, and Starr counties, the latter three of which are separated from Mexico by the Rio Grande River as it flows to the Gulf of Mexico. There are approximately 750,000 people living in the four counties. Willacy and Starr are rural, agricultural counties, while Cameron and Hidalgo counties are more developed in terms of business and industry. Brownsville, population 98,962, is in Cameron County; McAllen, population 84,021, is the largest city in Hidalgo County. The Martinez family lives in Starr County.

Visitors coming from more northerly climates in the U.S. know the Valley as a great place to visit to escape winter weather. The Rio Grande Valley Chamber of Commerce, located in McAllen, advertises the area's subtropical temperatures and the average January temperature of 60 degrees. The chamber also touts the balmy beaches along South Padre Island in the Gulf of Mexico, and the night life that can be enjoyed by crossing the border into Mexico. In the Valley, one can spot license plates from Colorado, the Dakotas, Wisconsin, Minnesota, Illinois, Iowa, Missouri, and numerous other northern states. Local residents call these people "Winter Texans," because they live here only during the winter months.

But what the tourist brochures will not point out are the problems found in the Valley. The migrant population's lifestyle, droughts, freezes, floods, the Texas deficit, and international problems such as the devaluation of the peso, all contribute to a high unemployment rate and an annual income that is far below the national average. According to the latest available statistics from the National Migrant Center in Austin, Texas, there were 114,485 migrant workers who called Hidalgo County their home in March 1990. Cameron County was the home base for 27,076; Starr County, 17,509; and Willacy County, 4,232.

(The center also said 7,469 migrant workers called Walla Walla County their home in March 1990. Other figures for Washington were: Columbia County, 139; Franklin County, 4,539; Benton County, 14,195; and Yakima County, 51,925. In Oregon, Morrow County had 2,459, and Umatilla County, 3,749.)

"For years, this area has been known as the 'home base' for migrant workers," Oliveira says. "Every spring they travel the country picking crops, then in the winter they come back here to work the citrus fruits. But work has been so scarce during the past three to four years because this area has suffered droughts, freezes, and floods."

U.S. representative Albert Bustamante agrees, saying that now, when migrants return home, they spend what they earned during harvest on bills incurred for necessities such as food, gas, and water. "And since they don't have any money left over, they have to buy everything on credit," Bustamante says. "So by the time the spring comes along, they're $300 in debt. So they have to go back out into the fields. It's an endless cycle."

"This is what they know, this is what they do, and they are very proud of it," Oliveira exclaims. "There is nothing wrong with it, because that is good, honest living. But through the years there is going to be less and less of a demand [for migrant workers] as agriculture becomes more mechanical and computerized."

There are a few solutions that Oliveira and Bustamante say could put an end to the migrant cycle. One is education and the other is the U.S.-Mexican Free Trade Agreement. For those who have the right education or training, "they can stay in one place and get a good paying job," Oliveira says.

"Right now what we are working on is getting migrant parents to understand the importance of a proper education," Oliveira points out. "This has to be the first step because many of these parents think an education isn't needed; instead, their children will work the fields."

Both agree the U.S.-Mexican Free Trade Agreement will allow big companies to open plants on Mexico's side of the border to capitalize on cheap labor. But, the lawmakers add, the agreement also will create jobs on the U.S. side because a lot of the supplies used to assemble products in Mexico are made in the United States.

"Although they may only be minimum-wage paying jobs, it will create some growth in the Valley and boost the economy," Oliveira notes.

But migrant workers have repeatedly said that minimum wage jobs are the only jobs available in the Valley, if there are any jobs at all. According to figures from the U.S. Department of Commerce, the 1990 average per capita income in Cameron County was $7,868; in Hidalgo County, $7,302; in Willacy County, $6,700; and in Starr County, $4,450. The unemployment rate in August 1991 in Cameron County was 11.9 percent, and 15.2 percent in Hidalgo County, according to the Texas Employment Commission. No figures were available for Starr and Willacy counties.

"We have a big problem on our hands, and the migrant workers are correct when they say there are no jobs or good paying jobs in the Valley," Oliveira admits. "But we're dealing with a lot of issues here. Texas had a $5 billion deficit that we are just starting to come out of, federal dollars are declining, and, since we are right on the border, Mexico's problems are our problems," the state representative says. "Mexico's peso devaluation really hurt us. This stopped Mexicans from crossing the border to this side to do their weekly shopping."

These are just a few of the difficulties facing the Texas border, Oliveira stresses. One of the state's current problems involves the small, unincorporated border communities, called "colonias," that have been in dire need of water and sewer services, and have been identified as breeding grounds for infectious diseases. In early November, voters agreed to let the state spend an additional $150 million for improvements in impoverished "colonias." The funds are expected to go a long way in addressing the needs of "colonia" residents, but some state officials estimate it will cost about $700 million to upgrade all such communities.

"When South Texas is not faced with one problem, it's faced with another. We don't know if we'll ever catch up," Oliveira says. "Colonias" began springing up along the border more than two decades ago, when developers carved up unused farmland and sold it cheap. Buyers, mostly immigrants and low-income families, were promised water and sewer service hookups that never came. An estimated 75,000 residents live in the 200 to 300 "colonias" in the Valley area. Overall, the state of Texas counts more than 200,000 residents in such communities, ranging along the border from El Paso to Brownsville.

Although the Valley is a wonderful destination for "Winter Texans" who travel yearly here to enjoy the subtropical temperatures, life for permanent residents can sometimes be anything but a vacation.

Life in LaGrulla

The word "grulla" means crane in Spanish. LaGrulla received its name from the flocks of whooping cranes that used to winter in the area. The community of 1,445 is similar to most of the towns in Starr County—rural, Hispanic in population, and lacking jobs, its biggest problem.

"Sixty percent of our population are migrant workers," notes city councilman Raymundo Gonzalez. "And the other 40 percent stay here and work in the local farms."

Local growers harvest cantaloupes, onions, bell peppers, watermelons, celery, oranges, and grapefruit. But the freezes, droughts, and floods that have plagued the South Texas Valley during the past three years have caused many farmers to go out of business.

"We're suffering an economic crunch right now. Many of the local farmers have gone bankrupt because people just aren't buying," Gonzalez says from his one-room office at his small, used-car lot.

"Just last year, one of our biggest farmers went under, he went bankrupt. He owned 5,000 acres and now he has nothing."

When migrant families such as the Martinezes return home for the winter after working the harvest in spring, summer, and fall, they look for jobs. "But lately, local work can't be found so they just live off unemployment," Gonzalez says. The Martinezes and the three children still at home live on about $900 a month in unemployment and Social Security benefits.

Life can be hard for families who have to pay taxes and utility bills, and buy food, gas, and clothing on the little income that they receive. "The biggest thing that kills people are taxes," Gonzalez points out. "And unfortunately they keep going up every year."

Most residents of LaGrulla are homeowners. County taxes are assessed at $1.51 per $100 valuation, and school taxes at 76 cents per $100 valuation. (Property taxes in Washington and Oregon are computed differently, using a tax rate per $1,000 of assessed value.) The average home in LaGrulla is worth only $8,000, making the total taxes about $182.

Another major complaint from LaGrulla residents is the cost of indoor plumbing. The price for connecting a water line to a home is $600 within the city limits, and $800 outside the city limits.

"We realize it's a big expense, but those $600 cover parts and labor, water rights, and the water meter, so the high cost is unavoidable," Gonzalez explains. "Even if they do complain, everyone has water."

Gonzalez, a lifetime resident of LaGrulla, says he has not seen the city grow much during his 55 years here. Records show that the 1980 census recorded 1,442 citizens in the town. Eleven years later that number had increased by three.

And, like all communities, there is crime in LaGrulla, which has no police force. Rather, the community is patrolled daily by one officer from the Starr County Sheriff's Department.

"We do have problems with crime, the biggest problem being drugs," Gonzalez admits, but he would not elaborate.

Despite all the difficulties that the residents of LaGrulla face, it is home. While over half of them leave their homes each spring in search of work elsewhere in the country, they, like the whooping cranes, return to LaGrulla for the winter. And, despite their repeated comments that there is "nothing" in LaGrulla, it is home to the Martinezes.

The town sits three miles south of Texas 83, a main highway connecting the cities and communities lining the South Texas border. Once Texas 83 is reached from LaGrulla, a 10-mile drive east or west is necessary before reaching a larger community. In LaGrulla, there are two "Mom and Pop" grocery stores, similar to general stores. But locals often won't shop there because, they say, prices are too high. Instead they drive into one of the larger communities to do their weekly shopping at a supermarket.

There are only two gas stations in LaGrulla. But again, residents say prices are too high.

There is an elementary school, a post office, two cemeteries, two churches – one Catholic and the other Mennonite – and a tiny park and community center, both of which are rarely used. A few businesses – two mini-markets and an auto shop – have closed during the past year after being open only one year.

The roads in the community are paved, but only wide enough for one car. The homes, mostly built of wood, are constructed closely together. It's common to see dogs and chickens cross the road, and, occasionally, tarantulas and rattlesnakes as well. In the mornings, residents are awakened by the crowing of roosters.

At night, the community is very dark, with a street light located every mile or so. Rarely does one see a front or back porch light on. During the day, most of the activity, and gossip, occurs at the post office. But usually the community is deserted as most of its residents go into Rio Grande City, 13 miles away, to do their business.

"The community has really gotten quiet, especially this year," Maria Elena says while sitting at her dining table, sipping coffee. "It used to be so lively. You would go outside and you could see everyone walking around, visiting neighbors, the teens driving by in beautiful trucks, and everyone would gather together. I don't know what happened, but things are so different, so sad. Things aren't the same no more."

Raul and Maria Elena were raised in LaGrulla, and Raul says the town is nothing like it was when he and his wife were married 35 years ago.

"Every weekend, there would be a dance at the center, when it was cold, or outside in the park when it was hot," he says in Spanish. "It used to cost us only $1 per person and everyone went with their entire families. Now, when there is a dance, you have to go all the way to Rio Grande City and it costs about $10 a person. Who around here has that kind of money?" he asks his wife. There also used to be a movie theater, but it has been closed for at least 15 years.

"Things have gotten real bad here," Maria Elena says. "I guess it's because there is no money."

Even though the economy has caused the community to lose much of the spirit it once had, the Martinezes say they will never leave their hometown.

"This is our home. This is where we were born, grew up, got married, and where our children were born," Maria Elena says. "How can you leave your home?"

Raul nods his head in agreement.

A House, A Home

Home is something that preoccupies the thoughts of most migrant workers, and to them the word means far more than a place on a map. As they work in the fields, they envision the time they can return home to find adequate paying jobs. They envision the day their children will no longer have to work in the fields. And they envision having a permanent place to live. For most of the migrant families who reside in the South Texas Valley, their biggest hope is owning their own house. To have a place of their own is something that makes them walk with pride.

Although Raul Jr. and his wife Iris spend most of the year in Boardman, and Iris has many times been offered a permanent job at the Child Development Center, the couple say they will never leave the South Texas Valley to move to the Pacific Northwest.

"It's too far from our families," Iris explains. "I don't think we could ever be that far away from them. Besides, it's too cold up there. I don't think we could stand it."

For the past three years, the couple has been using the money they earned to build their home in Mission, located about 26 miles east of LaGrulla. The house is expected to be completed in another three years.

"The first year we bought the land, the next year we laid the slab of cement, and last year we laid the bricks making the wall around the house," says Raul Jr. "This year we're putting on the roof, designing the interior of the house, and putting up the wood beams."

The work being done this year cost the couple $3,000, which they earned in Boardman. "Next year we'll work on laying the brick on the outside, then the next year we'll work on the plumbing and put in the windows and doors. Then we'll be able to move in the following year."

The home is being built by Raul Jr., and his brothers and brothers-in-law. Meanwhile, the couple and their 5-year-old daughter, Abby, live in the two-car garage adjacent to the house. Raul Jr. converted the garage into their temporary home, and Iris has it decorated comfortably. They have indoor plumbing, and the garage is big enough for a kitchen with dining table and china cabinet, a bedroom complete with bed, dressers, and television set, a small bathroom, and a place for their washer and dryer.

Having to wait three more years to move into their home is not a burden on the family. Over the years, they have learned that they must continue to work and slowly get what they want. However, Iris cannot help but get excited when visitors arrive. She quickly takes them to the house and walks them through it, pointing out where the various rooms will be located. The home will have three bedrooms, 1½ bathrooms, kitchen and dining room, and a laundry area. Of the three bedrooms, one is the master bedroom, the other is for Abby, and the third will be for their next child. Iris, two months pregnant, is due to have her baby next summer while in Boardman.

"The house is something I've always wanted," Iris says. "When we were first married, we lived with my parents. But then we decided we wanted our own home. So this is what we work for every time we go to Boardman, to save enough money to come home and add a little more to our house."

Iris also points out that it is helpful, and less expensive, to have her brothers and brothers-in-law help build the home. One of her brothers-in-law, Christobal Saenz, is a construction worker. Saenz built his own house in Mission for his wife and family.

"We all try to help each other any way we can, especially the young ones that are just starting off," Iris says. "That's what everyone wants, everyone works for, and everyone looks forward to—having their families and their own homes."

A 20-Year Investment

For the Barreras, the dream finally came true. For the past 20 years, Sam and Fedencia Barrera and their children have worked in the fields to make a better life for themselves. The Barreras and their three sons and a daughter have traveled to Walla Walla, Pasco, and other places in the Northwest to work the harvest before returning to the South Texas Valley, where they have built a home. Within the past 20 years, their house has grown from a crowded four rooms, to a more spacious, seven-room home.

"Not one nickel from Texas has been used to build this house. Every penny that has gone into the house was earned up north," Fedencia says in Spanish, somewhat resentful that there aren't enough jobs locally for the family to earn a living. "All the money we've earned has come from Pasco, where we pick asparagus; Walla Walla, where we've worked in the onion fields; and in Idaho, where we've also worked onion and the hop crops."

Fedencia, 48, and her 58-year-old husband are natives of Mexico and became U.S. citizens in 1970, which is when they first started their annual migrations to the Northwest. Her children—Sam, 28; Iris Martinez, 26, who also is a daughter-in-law of Raul and Maria Elena Martinez; Cesar, 23; and Hector, 22—spent most of their childhood in Walla Walla.

"We started taking our children there since they were very little. At the time there were no child labor laws and we took Hector at the age of 3 to work with us in the onion fields," Fedencia recalls. "We taught him how to hold the knife and how to grab one onion at a time and cut it."

Like all migrant workers, their days began at dawn and continued until after sunset. While in Walla Walla, Sam worked all day in the onion fields, while Fedencia returned to the Walla Walla Farm Labor Camp to prepare meals for her family. Then, from 1:30 to 4 p.m. she worked as a cook at ABC Taco, then went to work as a seamstress for a small company located at the Walla Walla Regional Airport.

"This was daily. I don't think my children ever ate a warm meal. I would cook in the mornings or at noon for the entire day," Fedencia says. "While we were at work, the children were at the day care center at the labor camp until they were old enough to come work with us in the fields, and that was usually at the age of 7 or so."

The Barrera family has a lot of memories of Walla Walla. About six photo albums are filled with pictures of their children celebrating birthdays at the labor camp, attending events at the day care center, working in the fields, and enjoying a day off at Pioneer Park. All the hard work, the traveling, and constant relocation has proved beneficial for the family, Fedencia says.

"Little by little, we've been able to build our house. We started off in 1973 when we bought the land for $300, which at that time was still a lot of money. And every year we've added more and more," she recalls. "Now the money we earn will be used to fix up the outside."

It's taken 20 years for Fedencia to have the house she's always wanted. Her home, which is located about four miles outside of LaGrulla, is decorated with curtains and bedspreads that Fedencia has made. She also earns money sewing for people during the winter.

"I'm very proud of my home because it's all made by hand and built from hard-earned money." But the thing she is most proud of, she says, is letting people know that migrant families can have beautiful homes.

"Many people think that we are used to living in three-room homes, without furniture, and everyone crowded together," Fedencia exclaims. "We may live like that when we are working throughout the country, or when we're living in labor camps. But we live that way out of necessity, not because we want to or because we're used to it. When we come home, we come to our nice homes and we continue putting some of the money we've earned to make our homes even better."

Folk Customs

One of the predominant aspects of the Rio Grande Valley is the rich South Texas folklore derived from the Indian, Spanish, and Mexican cultures. Some of these traditions are practiced in Hispanic communities throughout the country. The most obvious custom—because it can readily be seen along highways in the Valley—is the placing of funeral wreaths or decorative crosses where loved ones have died. If someone dies in a car or train accident, a wreath, cross, or some other symbol is placed on the exact location to let others know where the person was when his soul left his body. These memorials, usually found near heavy traffic, dangerous intersections, or railroad crossings, are maintained year-round. All along the highway to LaGrulla, wreaths and crosses are visible. When driving past one, Maria Elena Martinez or other family members will reminisce about who died there and when.

Folk medicines also are commonly utilized. Popular among Mexicans and Hispanics alike is the medicinal uses of "hierba buena," the "good herb." Commonly used for colds, "hierba buena" is said to flourish only in the gardens of wives who dominate their households. The "manzanilla," whose leaves are widely used to brew tea as a remedy for stomach ailments, is said to grow and produce its red berries only in gardens where the husbands are the undisputed head of the house. In labor camps in Walla Walla or Milton-Freewater, it is not uncommon to see people knocking on their neighbor's door asking for "manzanilla" or "heirba buena." In many cases, the use of such teas is highly preferred over a visit to the doctor.

Some illnesses, however, cannot be cured simply by drinking a cup of tea. An illness or misfortune brought on by "mal puesto" or "ojo"—the Evil Eye—is a different matter, requiring different treatment. The evil may not be intentional. An admiring glance, unless accompanied by a friendly touch, may bring on something evil in the form of an illness. Mild cases are cured by simply placing a bottle of water on the pillow to absorb the evil. An egg, broken in a saucer and placed under the victim's bed, might lump together as the fever goes down, effecting a cure.

"Susto" is a mental state brought on by some shock or misfortune. "Curanderos," people who have special powers to heal, use various methods to restore mental health. Prayers are a common treatment, often accompanied by sweeping motions of a broom while the patient lies outstretched upon a cross of ashes. These are a few of the common traditions that keep Hispanic families bonded together no matter how far away from home they are.

Day of the Dead

The first traditional event the Martinez family celebrates after arriving home is "Dia de los Muertos," or Day of the Dead—a traditional Hispanic custom. In many Hispanic communities throughout the United States, "Dia de los Muertos" is commemorated on November 2—a day set aside to honor and remember departed loved ones. On Saturday morning, November 2, Raul and Maria Elena awake early to go into "el pueblo" to purchase colorful, decorative funeral wreaths. Later, they proceed to the cemetery to clean up the grave of Maria Elena's father and place a wreath on the plot.

"My mother reminded me last night about 'Dia de los Muertos,' " Maria Elena says. "She told me, 'You don't even remember your poor father anymore.' "

"Dia de los Muertos" is a centuries-old Indian/Hispanic tradition, blending pagan and Roman Catholic beliefs. It dates back to before the coming of Columbus, when native people accepted death as a natural transition from life, honoring their dead in ceremonies sometimes lasting months.

On this day, relatives of those who have died prepare altars with "ofrendas" in their honor. The altars, which are usually placed in the home, exhibit things the people enjoyed while alive. "Ofrendas" usually include the loved one's photo, the person's favorite food and drink, candles, cigarettes, and marigolds—the traditional flower of the dead. Other traditional items are sugar "calaveras," fruit punch, and "pan de muerto," a traditional Day of the Dead bread.

At the grave sites, relatives of the dead clear away weeds, rake and sweep, and put out fresh flowers. Some families spend the entire day at the graves, and Mass sometimes is celebrated in these Catholic cemeteries.

"We will clean up around the grave and place floral wreaths, but it's not too big of a tradition in our family," Maria Elena says. "But for a lot of people around here it is. You should see the cemetery on that day. It looks so beautiful with all the flowers and ribbons."

Maria Elena and Raul are the only members of their family who have decided to pay a visit to the grave site; however, Charlie decides to stop by later to see his grandfather's grave. "I like to come by sometimes, but not too often," Charlie comments, not giving further explanation. At the cemetery he looks around, seeing others cleaning grave sites. He walks around reading tombstones, fixes flowers on his grandfather's grave, then quietly leaves.

Two Churches, Two Views, One Town

There are two churches in this community of 1,445 – one Catholic, the other Mennonite. One church has become the voice of the people, while the other is more concerned with spiritual matters. But no matter what position each has taken, both have strong followings.

For about the past 10 years, Jose Gonzalez Diaz has been preaching "the Bible" at the Mennonite church. He first began preaching to migrant workers in Gresham, Oregon, and five years ago he and his wife, Cindy, and their three children moved to the South Texas Valley. He has been the minister here in LaGrulla for the past four years.

The Rev. Lee DaCosta has been a Catholic priest in the Valley since 1969, when he first entered the priesthood. He has helped many Central and South American immigrants who have come to this country in search of a better life – from finding them shelter, to assisting them in obtaining citizenship. DaCosta became pastor of Holy Family Catholic Church five months ago. Some members of the Martinez family are members of the Mennonite church, while others are Catholic.

"During the six years that I was living in Oregon, my job was different. There I would go out into the fields and the labor camps and read the Bible to the workers," Gonzalez recalls. "There I did help people with material things such as food and clothing that was donated to my church by other churches. But here, my work is primarily to teach the people the teachings of the Bible. I want people to recognize what is true in the Bible."

Gonzalez says his church in LaGrulla gives Bibles to people who come to see him so that they may learn the "word of God and how he wants us to live." Originally from Mexico City, Gonzalez's goal is to return to his homeland someday and begin a church there. "But right now my work is here," he says. "There are a lot of people who need spiritual healing and are thirsty for the word of God. That is why I will continue to stay here for as long as necessary."

Mennonites are a Protestant group known for emphasizing plain ways of dressing, living, and worshiping. There are many branches of Mennonites; however, those who live in rural areas tend to dress and live much more simply than those in urban areas. The Mennonite church in LaGrulla has a congregation of 80 people, and there are four other Mennonite churches located throughout the Valley. They were established about 40 years ago.

More than half of the residents of LaGrulla belong to the Catholic church. "Our job is to facilitate the people," DaCosta says. "With respect to the migrants, we are here to perform baptisms or weddings before or after they leave to look for work elsewhere. Some of the other Catholic churches in the Valley will hold special Masses for them in the spring before they leave."

DaCosta is a firm believer that the duty of the Catholic church is not simply to be a spiritual voice, but a voice for the people as well. As the years go by, the church is finding itself more involved in political activities.

"There's nothing wrong with being politically active," DaCosta notes. "Jesus Christ was very politically minded. He was a crusader for social justice." DaCosta continues: "Just because someone is poor, or comes from Mexico and works the fields, that doesn't mean they should be denied their rights."

DaCosta, a native of Brazil, says he understands oppression. "But this is not Mexico or some other country where priests are not allowed to voice their opinion or fight. I know there is a separation between church and state, but that does not mean we have to keep quiet," he exclaims. "I try to teach people, that they have rights, they have a voice, and that people have power."

DaCosta is known throughout the Valley as an advocate for human rights. Throughout the past decade, he has worked for the rights of undocumented pregnant women and juveniles from Latin American countries who were detained by the United States Border Patrol and placed in city or county jails.

"How can these people be put in jail? They have done nothing wrong, but there was nowhere else to put them," he says. So DaCosta helped find them temporary shelters with local families, or secured money to get these people back with their families. "Other priests and the Border Patrol used to call my house 'Casa de Amistad' [House of Friendship] because of the work I did," he says. Since then, DaCosta's involvement in this regard has slowly decreased because the Border Patrol now has facilities where these people can be placed temporarily instead of in jails.

"But what I'm still finding with people in this part of the country, whether they are documented or not, is that many are intimidated, scared, or don't know they have rights. And so they come to the church, and who better than the church to help them strive for justice. Someone has to speak for them. If no one speaks, nothing will get done. These people need a voice, a leader. Someone to show them and tell them what to do. And I don't think there is anything wrong with the Catholic Church doing that."

About 20 years ago, some members of the Martinez family, including Maria Elena and Raul, left the Catholic church and became Mennonites. "I saw that the Catholic church was always getting after the kids if they were making too much noise in church, or they criticized people and embarrassed them right in front of everyone," Maria Elena recalls. "I stopped going to that church, and I began to see other people going to the Mennonite church, so I started going. Then Raul joined me and then we started taking all the kids."

The older Martinez children have remained in the Catholic church, while the younger ones, along with their parents, are members of the Mennonite church. "I really don't know why my parents switched religions. I guess it works for them, but I'm comfortable with the Catholic church and that's what I want to follow," their daughter Ellen Herbert says.

Once last summer in Boardman, Maria told me that what she liked most about the Mennonite religion was the teaching of the Bible. "In the Catholic church I never read the Bible like I am now," she says. There were many evenings when I would see Maria Elena grab a Bible and sit outside our apartment complex to read. That usually prompted her children to join her. Later, other migrant families living nearby would gather and a Bible discussion would begin. I sat in on some of the discussions and found them interesting. I liked seeing the expressions on their faces when they would come across a psalm or proverb that made reference to laborers or harvesting.

Maria Elena says, "I think that is why we have always been blessed in finding work and even when we are not working, because the Bible always mentions that those who work hard in the harvest season will not suffer in the winter. I truly believe that, and that God will take care of us—all the migrant workers."

I met many migrant families while I was living in Washington and Oregon, and in each household I visited there was a cross or statue placed somewhere, or a picture of Jesus Christ adorning a wall. Sometimes I attended the Spanish Mass at St. Patrick Catholic Church, where I saw many of the migrant families from the Walla Walla and Milton-Freewater labor camps. I learned that religion plays a very important role in their lives. No matter how far away they are from their homes and families, they always have their religion—and faith—with them. When an infant is born, the talk within the family is about the baptism the child will have when they get home. And in those times when the work has taken its toll on everyone, and they feel they can no longer endure the pain and they are worried about how they will make it through the winter, someone is always heard saying, "Don't worry. God will help you."

None ever spoke about how the church should assist them financially or with material goods. That wasn't expected. What they looked for from the church was spiritual guidance. All said, they received that from their church, regardless of which religion it was.

Tejano: Music of the People

Before the 1980s, the term "Tejano music," if used at all, was classed with a number of other terms applied to the music created by Mexican-American musicians of South Texas. It has been performed for decades, but no one had attempted to coin a universal term for it. There was "conjunto music," "mariachi music," "polka music," "cumbias," "rancheras," even "brown-eyed soul." But all of it was usually lumped under the term "Mexican music."

But over the years, musicians and audiences realized that the term "Mexican music" did not apply, primarily because the vast majority of artists creating Tejano music were not Mexican. They were Americans of Mexican descent, who borrowed from everywhere, including traditional Mexican and Spanish forms, for their musical inspiration. But those two aspects did not make it "Mexican music."

The literal translation of the word "Tejano" means "Texan," but in South Texas it means "Texan of Mexican descent." In the same respect, the term "Tejano music" has come to mean "Texas music of Mexican descent."

Rudy Trevino and Gilbert Escobedo, San Antonians who are historians of Tejano music and originators of the televised Tejano Music Awards, are probably most responsible for the term "Tejano music."

"The best way to describe Tejano music is 'music of the people,' " Trevino explains. "It is the influence of our culture and the influence of our bilingualism. It brings people together, and no matter what part of the country you are in, when you listen to it you get a feeling of home." Trevino says Tejano music has a style of its own because it is more a frame of mind.

"But one thing is for sure, Tejano music is dancing music. You cannot just sit there and listen to it. It makes you want to get up and dance."

Although Tejano music is influenced by German polkas, Trevino and others say, not all Tejano music sounds alike. Some groups sound like traditional "conjunto," which is virtually dominated by the button accordion. Other groups are influenced by the ballad tradition. A third category can be called "augmented conjuntos," with the accordion still present, or with a synthesizer imitating an accordion, but with a much more traditional rhythm section that includes electric bass and drums. No matter what sound is preferred, Tejano music has grown in popularity throughout the country.

"The music originated in South Texas, but can now be heard in Michigan, California, Idaho, Washington, Oregon, Arizona, Ohio, Nevada, New Mexico, and Florida. And this can be highly attributed to the migrant circuit," Trevino says. "Since its roots began in South Texas decades ago and it is music of the people with its own original sound, it travels with our people," Trevino further explains. "The music follows the migrant worker and more often than not will settle in the communities where the migrants work."

Radio station KSMX, the only Spanish-language station in the Walla Walla Valley, plays many recordings by Tejano artists. Salvador Hernandez, the station's disc jockey, notes that listeners currently request a mixture of music, including salsa, "merengue," and music from Mexico.

"But I think that come May, when Texans return to the area again to work, we will probably start getting more requests for Tejano music. And that should continue through October or so," Hernandez says.

The popularity of Tejano music has not only grown to the extent that radio stations throughout the country are playing it, but artists who perform Tejano music are now being recognized nationally. Even the Grammy Awards has a special category honoring Tejano artists.

"We knew Tejano music was very popular and these artists were very talented, but they were getting nowhere. They were not getting the recognition they deserved," Trevino says.

Then, in 1980, Trevino and Escobedo held the first Tejano Music Awards. The budget for the show was $15,000, contributed entirely by Anheuser-Busch. The show took place in the ballroom of a San Antonio hotel, and was presented live on a local Spanish television station.

The projected cost for the 1992 awards program was about $475,000, provided by Anheuser-Busch, along with Coca-Cola, R.J. Reynolds, and the San Antonio Light newspaper. Trevino estimated 13 million viewers nationwide on simulcast, with 14,500 attending the program at the San Antonio Convention Center Area.

"Many people travel in buses from as far away as Washington and Florida. Radio stations all over really promote the show and some travel agents have discounts," Trevino says. The Tejano Music Awards is similar to the Grammy awards in that there are celebrity hosts and musical performances, but that is where the similarities end. Whereas other awards are presented in only English, Tejano hosts switch back and forth between English and Spanish, rapidly speaking to a crowd that understands both.

Whether Tejano music can maintain its present popularity remains to be seen, but Trevino says it is important for the Tejano spirit to remain alive within the Tejano people, and be carried with them wherever they go. And that, Trevino believes, will never die. Music, especially Tejano music, creates a special bond between the migrant workers and former migrants who have settled in the Walla Walla area.

While living with migrant families in Walla Walla and Boardman, I noticed that they look for signs of things they have in common with other migrants. One of the first things they notice when driving through a labor camp or migrant community is the car license plates. Jimmy and Charlie will quickly point out to their mother when a car is from Texas. "Look mom, they're from Texas, too," one of the boys will say.

But the most important bond is music. Every home at the labor camp has a radio, and the music that is heard is usually Tejano music. Most migrant workers will carry cassette tapes of Tejano music with them wherever they travel; sometimes they will listen to it while working in the fields. At night after work—but primarily on Saturday nights— many migrant workers will gather around their cars at the labor camps to talk, drink beer, and enjoy music.

Radio stations in Walla Walla and Pasco occasionally bring a popular Tejano group to perform in the area. These dances attract a large number of Hispanics, regardless of whether or not they are migrant workers. I remember a dance I attended at the Southeastern Washington Fairgrounds, with admission at $30 per person. To my amazement I saw many people — young and old, even children — from the Walla Walla and Milton-Freewater labor camps.

Music is very important to the Martinez family, and Maria Elena always has Tejano music playing in the kitchen. When I first moved in with them, she asked who my favorite group was and if I liked a certain song. Charlie's way of communicating is through music, and he loves Tejano music. I prefer country music over Tejano, and he knows that. When he is upset with me, he puts a Tejano music tape on his cassette recorder and plays it real loud while I am trying to read or write. If he wants to show that he likes me, he turns on country music. When I turn on my car after he's borrowed it, I notice that all the stations are programmed to Tejano radio stations, but he'll apologize for it.

When I first arrived in Walla Walla I was surprised to learn how popular Tejano music was. I heard it on KSMX radio; I heard it played in people's homes; and I saw the large crowds Tejano music artists attracted. A migrant worker once told me that listening to Tejano music takes him back home. Tejano music, although I don't care for it too much, does give a sense of "home."

Chapter 9

Illegal Aliens, Drug Smugglers, and the Border Patrol

S INCE I WAS A CHILD growing up in Central Texas, I remember hearing stories about U.S. Border Patrol agents—usually Anglo and over 6 feet tall—verbally and physically harassing illegal aliens, especially those from Mexico. But because I hadn't witnessed such harassment, I never formed an opinion. All I knew was that its agents dealt with illegal aliens; and since I am a U.S. citizen, they did not have any business with me.

Now, while spending an eight-hour shift with an agent, the Border Patrol is earning my respect and admiration. It is mid-January and I am accompanying Agent Bryan Langham, a four-year veteran on the force, on his 3 to 11 p.m. shift. I learn that agents have to work under all weather conditions, day or night, and put their lives in danger. At the same time, they show compassion for impoverished people who illegally enter the United States in search of a better life.

The day is beautiful and sunny, with temperatures in the 60s. But rains plaguing the area days before have left the ground muddy. During the first hours of Langham's shift, while there is daylight, we drive up and down the river bordering the United States and Mexico. The section of the Rio Grande that he monitors extends from McAllen to the tiny community of Pharr, about four miles east. Heavy brush lines the river banks, and I am amazed at how Langham can determine whether someone has walked through the area just moments before we get there. He studies footprints and broken tree limbs, and is aided by electronic sensors the Border Patrol uses to detect movement at selected spots along the river bank.

At one stop, he hears soft murmurs in the distance and follows the barely audible voices. Langham slows his pace and softens his footsteps as he makes his way through the thick, calf-high brush. I follow close behind. Langham crouches near the embankment and spots three men. They are speaking in Spanish, but I can't hear what they are saying. He races toward them, but the men jump in the river. Langham leaps down to the embankment and climbs on a tree limb over the river.

"Hey, come back," he shouts in Spanish. "Where are you going? How's the water?" he asks, jokingly. The three men keep swimming toward the Mexican side. Langham notices a fresh pack of cigarettes. He picks them up. "Your cigarettes. You left your cigarettes here," he shouts.

"They're for you. We left them for you," one replies as the three men finally reach the other side and crawl out of the water.

Langham throws the cigarettes in the water and climbs back up the embankment, laughing. "They'll be back later tonight. Those were bandits." Langham says bandits are either U.S. or Mexican citizens who sit at the edge of the river on the U.S. side, waiting for illegal aliens to rob or rape.

He tells a story of a 14-year-old girl being gang raped. "That was hard to deal with. That's when I find this job difficult, when I come upon something like that," Langham says. "She had already been through enough, and then she still had to go through our questioning and processing."

We return to the Border Patrol's drab green truck, which is similar to a paddy wagon, and drive along the edge of the river until we see children playing along the Mexican side. When they spot us they start shouting, jumping, and waving their arms. "Over there! Mister, there's one over there!" they shout at us in Spanish while pointing at the U.S. side of the river. Langham stops to look, then starts laughing at them, knowing that the children are kidding him. This continues for some time before the children begin shouting profanities at us. Langham continues laughing and taunting them for a while.

"They love cussing at us. They do this all the time they see us," he says as we drive off.

As nighttime falls, so does the temperature. Langham returns to his station to equip himself with night-vision binoculars. When we head back to the river, we receive a report that there is some heavy foot traffic near us. Langham radios in that we are headed in that direction. With headlights turned off, the vehicle crosses darkened fields, brush, and ditches. Langham is asked if he has his partner with him. "No. I have a reporter with me," he answers over the radio.

"OK, we'll be listening for you and we're headed out that direction to give you backup," the voice on the two-way responds.

We park the truck. It is about 8 p.m., and the only light we have is that of a half-moon. "I want you to put my jacket on," Langham instructs me. Temperatures have dipped to the 40s.

"We're going to go out and wait for them. If they're illegals, then we'll get them. If they have guns, we'll return to the vehicle and catch them farther down," he says. (Langham was making sure he avoided dangerous confrontations only because he didn't want to endanger me.)

We get out of the truck and make our way through brush, trees, rocks, mud, and ditches until we arrive at the place where Langham expects the illegal aliens to approach. It is a farmer's field, and a line of trees stand in the distance. Barbed wire separates us from the field. We wait in silence, with Langham looking through his binoculars, and the night vision binoculars we picked up at the station. He hands me binoculars every so often to look through. In the darkness, we rely on our ears, listening for voices and footsteps. Instead we hear dogs barking in the distance and the sounds of various animals that roam at night.

After 45 minutes of tense waiting, we and our backup unit decide to catch them at a different location. "It's obvious they're not going to come through here. They must have gone another direction," Langham explains.

We return to the vehicle and drive around the area. Langham returns to where the illegals were first detected, and gets out to study footprints. When he returns to the truck, he calls on the radio, "There's four of them, two males, a female, and a child." We continue tracing their tracks until they disappear. "They must have headed into the brush," he says, and he calls in the information.

This is in the Pharr section of Langham's beat. We decide to return to the international border crossing at McAllen because Langham's partner, Brent De Leon, has apprehended two illegal aliens. Earlier in the evening, De Leon picked up another two, both boys, ages 14 and 17. The youths were asked their names, addresses, parents' names, and whether they wanted to return to Mexico voluntarily or go before a judge. If they chose the latter, they would be detained. They chose returning voluntarily and were placed in the rear of the truck.

"How many times have you been caught?" Langham asked in Spanish as we drive them to the International Bridge.

"Four times this week," one replied. It is only Tuesday.

When we arrive at the bridge, Langham lets them out. "Be good. I don't want to see you guys over here anymore," he told them.

"No, not anymore tonight. It's cold and I don't want to cross the river because I may get pneumonia," one said as they started across the bridge into Mexico.

By now it is 10 p.m. — one more hour left in Langham's shift. We decide to park the truck and wait for something to happen. The night is slow, Langham keeps telling me. Only 20 illegal aliens have been picked up along the entire 100-mile stretch of the Rio Grande that Langham, De Leon, and eight other agents patrol. Usually twice that number are caught.

As we sit here waiting in the dark, my mind keeps wandering back to those stories I heard as a child. I look at Langham and the men he works with, and I see just the opposite. These men are compassionate to illegal aliens, giving them advice, in some cases providing them with money, and in many cases sympathizing with them.

"We're human and I don't think any one of us could turn our heads to a woman holding a crying child because of hunger, or to a youth who is over here looking for work to help support his family in Mexico. But we have a job to do and there's laws we have to respect, and that's why we're here," Langham says.

The Border Patrol

The U.S. Border Patrol has grown substantially since its founding more than 70 years ago, but its mission and the primary problems it faces along the Mexican border remain much the same. In its infancy, the Border Patrol first sought to stop an influx of Asians and Europeans who entered the United States illegally, and who often used burro pack trains to smuggle liquor into the country. Then the Asians and Europeans were replaced by Mexicans, and the liquor smugglers were replaced by narcotics smugglers.

The Border Patrol is a branch of the U.S. Immigration and Naturalization Service. In 1921, its first year, the Border Patrol had but four agents in the Rio Grande Valley. Today it has 324 officers working 17,000 square miles that embrace 19 counties in the southernmost tip of Texas alone.

There are five border stations from Rio Grande City west to Brownsville, and two coastal stations and two checkpoint sections located about 100 miles north of the Mexican border. Agents patrol this area in 4-wheel-drive vans and helicopters, on horseback, motor bikes, or dirt bikes, and at times on foot. During the day, agents can work alone; at night, they operate in teams.

Illegal aliens who cross the border in daylight usually come to steal or are seeking work, Bryan Langham says, whereas a lot of those who come at night are transporting drugs. Agents note that there are certain times when illegal aliens try to cross the border in greater numbers.

"The holiday season is always heavy because they return home for the holidays. Then when the holidays are over, they start coming back. March, April, and May are also heavy because that is when a lot of them come to work in the fields," Langham explains.

The number of illegal aliens caught by the Border Patrol in the McAllen sector was 97,018 in 1990. In 1991, that number decreased to 87,319. Agents say going after illegal aliens can be just as dangerous as trying to catch drug traffickers. According to Langham, about four years ago illegals were placing booby traps in the thick brush.

"They would place boards with nails on them so we could step on them, or they would tie rocks on the hanging branches so that when our vans would go by the rocks would crack the windshields," he explains.

"The problem [of illegal aliens] is running so rampant that we need to have 24-hour surveillance of the river," says Mario Garcia Jr., the Border Patrol's supervisory intelligence agent in McAllen. "And even then, we can't get them all."

Langham says the busiest places for illegal crossings are near the ports of entry. "And the perfect time for crossing is on cold, rainy, stormy nights. When it's a miserable night, it is a perfect night." Those who cross after midnight and before the break of dawn are the most dangerous, he notes.

The Border Patrol deals with both individual illegal aliens, coming to the U.S. to steal or seek work, and entire families, who come in search of a better life. "We also have so many pregnant women who come over here so their babies can be born U.S. citizens. We had one woman whose water broke on the Mexican side and then she swam over here so her baby could be born in the states," Langham recalls.

And the people crossing the river are no longer only from Mexico. They also come from Central and South America, Asia, and even the Middle East, Garcia says. And more and more of those people, no matter where the country of origin, come carrying drugs.

A Drug Smuggler's Paradise

Officials consider the border area in the southernmost tip of Texas a smuggler's paradise. They claim that for years, a sophisticated drug distribution system has mushroomed, making the Valley the main artery for drugs flowing into the United States from Mexico. A decade ago, Miami was the main point of entry for narcotics from South America. Today, South Texas is the hot spot.

The Border Patrol is increasingly busy trying to stop drug trafficking in the McAllen sector. In 1990, agents in the area seized drugs valued at $158 million in 935 narcotic cases. In 1991 that number increased to 1,035 cases, with drugs valued at $206 million. One of the most recent cases involved seizure of 7,343 pounds of marijuana on January 13 at the Border Patrol's traffic checkpoint about 60 miles north of McAllen. The marijuana, seized from a propane tanker-trailer driven by a 38-year-old U.S. citizen, was valued at about $5 million.

"The lives of our agents are constantly placed in danger of armed assault," says Garcia. But the number of armed encounters in the McAllen sector has actually decreased by 64 percent recently. There were 72 armed encounters in 1990, and 46 in 1991. Border Patrol agents receive training yearly, and use modern and sophisticated equipment to combat drug trafficking and the smuggling of illegal aliens.

"This is a never-ending job and the agents are constantly learning," Garcia says. "And that's important because it seems like we're always dealing with a new type of smuggler."

Migrant Drug Smugglers

When the Martinez family and I were in the Pacific Northwest last summer and fall, I often spoke to migrant workers about their hometowns in the Texas Valley. I found it very interesting that one of the most common remarks was, "In the Valley, if you're not a migrant worker, you are a drug dealer." That's exaggerating the truth. But in the Texas Valley, the tiny community of LaGrulla has a notorious reputation for heavy drug trafficking.

My first knowledge of this came one night in Boardman, while I was talking with Maria Elena. She told me that many people from LaGrulla turn to selling drugs because there is so much money in it and because there are no jobs in the town.

"They know what it's like to work in the fields, and it's very hard. So they would rather get involved in drugs," she said.

One night I was talking to Charlie and he was telling me about the brand new, beautiful, fully-equipped trucks people drive in LaGrulla. "One day they don't have anything and the next day they have this big truck that costs thousands of dollars," he said.

"How do they get it?" I asked.

"Selling drugs," he replied matter-of-factly.

When we arrived in LaGrulla on October 31, Maria Elena noticed that the little community was quieter than normal. "I guess they [law enforcement officers] have picked up all the drug traffickers. Last year this place was so lively with trucks driving up and down the streets all the time," she said, sounding almost remorseful that the place had settled down a bit. Even the local minister and his wife remarked to me one day about how, years before, trucks could be heard driving up and down the main highway leading to LaGrulla. The drivers supposedly were dealing in drugs.

When I visited with U.S. Border Patrol agents recently, I told them I was living in LaGrulla. "Oh, you're sitting right in the middle of one of the heaviest places for drug trafficking," Brent De Leon said.

"LaGrulla is a highway for drugs," Langham pointed out. It is the only place the police department or sheriff's department will not enter without a Border Patrol backup team.

LaGrulla city officials are also quick to point out that the biggest problem facing the community is drugs. I ask City Councilman Raymundo Gonzalez, "If you know it's such a big problem and you claim to know those who are involved, why isn't something done about it?"

"There is. People are being picked up and now there is not a problem in comparison to what it was years ago," Gonzalez says. "I guess the reason you keep hearing all this is because that reputation hasn't left us."

That may be the case, but Maria Elena says she still fears her youngest children may want to get involved in drug dealing. "All they see is that it's easy money, so I'm constantly keeping my eye on them and looking at who they hang around with," she exclaims. "But I don't think they would get involved in that. The older [children] would be all over them if that ever happened."

Maria Elena's fears are not ungrounded. Many migrant workers in South Texas serve as "mules," a nickname given to the people who transport the drugs. Deliveries extend far to the north; drug activity in central Washington, particularly the Yakima area, is especially substantial, according to Drug Enforcement Administration agents. In Walla Walla, however, police say the number of cases have been few.

"We don't see the bulk of migrant workers that come up here as being drug dealers," says Terry Thompson, a sergeant with the police department. "The majority of the migrant workers coming up here are honest, hard-working people. There is a drug problem here in Walla Walla and that involves whites, Hispanics, and blacks. It is not concentrated to only one group. And most of these people are residents."

He further stated that although there are some migrant workers who are involved in drug dealing, the problem would still exist even if they were not in the area. "The police deal with a small number of Hispanics and blacks, but unfortunately they are the ones that get all the bad press," Thompson said.

Walla Walla police officers mentioned a case occurring about four years ago involving migrant workers from Mexico who traveled through California, Idaho, and up to Walla Walla working the fields. While traveling through those states, they made cocaine and marijuana deliveries.

"They had people established here in Walla Walla where they would do their drops," recalled Sergeant Thompson. "Those people that lived here helped honest migrant workers that came to work by providing them with housing, vehicles, and other things they needed – but with that came a price. These honest migrant workers also had to hide drugs in their homes." After months of investigation, police arrested those involved and the organized ring ceased.

Migrant workers say that making drops at various sites throughout the United States puts a significant amount of money in their pockets. Police officers from Brownsville note that the bulk-rate price of a kilogram of cocaine can start out as low as $8,000 in Matamoros, Mexico, sister-city to Brownsville. It increases to at least $18,000 when it crosses the Rio Grande into the United States; shoots up to $30,000 once it passes the Border Patrol highway checkpoints – sporadically located about 100 miles north of the Mexican border – and reaches $40,000 or more in Houston. The price keeps escalating the farther north the drugs are transported. Narcotic agents with the DEA in Brownsville say the value of the kilo may go up to $50,000 to $60,000 once it reaches Washington state.

Payment to transporters, or "mules," varies depending on their circumstances. For example, an illegal alien who does not have any money may get paid $600 to $1,000 for making a delivery.

"But for those who transport drugs in 18-wheelers and know the ropes, they may get paid $200 per pound of marijuana or $2,000 to $3,000 for every kilo of cocaine," says Rolando Vasquez, narcotics agent with the Brownsville Police Department. Vasquez points out that expert traffickers deliver thousands of pounds of marijuana and hundreds of kilos of cocaine. A "mule" who is an expert in transporting drugs may carry 7,000 pounds of marijuana and get paid $200 a pound, receiving $1.4 million when the delivery is made. By comparison, a migrant worker may earn $4,000 for six weeks of cutting asparagus.

A handful of migrant workers say that, with the value of drugs at such high levels, transporting narcotics into Washington state is a major priority. "Once you've taken drugs all the way to Washington and you don't get caught, it becomes that much easier for you to do it again the next year," one field worker says.

"The asparagus season is always the best time to transport drugs. We have to travel all the way to Washington to work, and sometimes the drugs are sold to the field workers to help them ease their pain," another migrant worker adds. Asparagus cutting is such a back-breaking job that over-the-counter drugs often do not ease the pain. However, few cutters use drugs because the price is extremely high. The current street value for a gram of cocaine is $60, while an ounce of cocaine sells for $600 to $800. There are about 28 grams to an ounce. The migrant workers who spoke on the subject did so on condition they remain anonymous for fear of retaliation.

"When you have people that are extremely poor, and [transporting drugs] is an easy way to make money, you can see why so many people are willing to take the risk," explains Mario Garcia Jr., the Border Patrol's supervisory intelligence agent in McAllen. "Besides, these people really have nothing to lose if they are caught," Garcia adds in a telephone interview.

According to law enforcement officers, drugs are transported through Mexico to the South Texas border by car or plane. Once at the border, the narcotics are smuggled across the Rio Grande in boats, hand-pulled ferries, or even on people's backs. Sometimes smugglers simply walk across the border at U.S. Customs ports of entry carrying drugs, such as cocaine or heroin, concealed on their body or in body cavities. Drugs that cross in tractor-trailers are hidden under produce, or in secret compartments, or buried in legitimate imports. Sometimes the drop-off points are in the southern parts of Texas; other times, drugs are delivered to various northern states. Because of this, the U.S. Border Patrol has checkpoints on all northbound Texas highways.

The greatest flow of drugs comes across the Rio Grande through Hidalgo, Cameron, and Starr counties. These three counties, of course, are separated from Mexico only by the Rio Grande as it flows to the Gulf of Mexico. There are approximately 750,000 people residing in these counties, including adjacent Willacy County. Brownsville and McAllen and their Mexican sister-cities of Matamoros and Reynosa, respectively, along with Starr County, which is sparsely populated and lined with thick brush, are a smuggler's haven.

"There are a lot of drugs that are brought through this area on plane, boats, on foot, cars, whatever," Garcia says. "And since Mexico is literally five blocks down the street from the United States, drug traffickers can run to either side and find refuge."

To the outsider, the South Texas Valley is like a country of its own. Residents speak their own language, termed Tex-Mex; the Mexican peso and the U.S. dollar are interchangeable, so it is like having their own currency; and, most importantly, anyone escaping arrest simply needs to cross to either side of the border. Narcotics agents are also quick to point out that virtually everyone along the South Texas border knows someone who is involved in drug dealing.

"The media will always ask, 'If you know there is so much dealing going on, why don't you do something about it?'" Bryan Langham says. "The problem is that these communities are so small that whenever a new car or new person moves into the area, everyone there knows about it. You can't make any moves without everybody knowing where you're going, where you're at, who you're talking to. These communities are such a tight-knit group that even if someone is not directly involved in drugs, they have a certain loyalty to one another. Undercover agents have a very hard time because there is no way they can be under cover."

People refuse to talk about drug dealings. Within the migrant communities, they know it takes place and who the dealers are, yet they never think about turning them over to authorities. That's because many of the authorities they would normally turn to are involved in drug smuggling themselves, according to Texas narcotic agents.

The tiny and most impoverished county—Starr County, population 36,473—also happens to be the most notorious in terms of having a corrupt image. Three recent court cases there prove this. The county clerk was sentenced to 5 1/4 years in prison for possession of marijuana and money laundering. A justice of the peace received 2½ years for trying to sell 121 pounds of marijuana to undercover officers, and a constable was convicted for possession and conspiracy to distribute marijuana.

"Who do we go to?" one migrant worker asks. "Everyone is involved in drugs. You say something, they kill you."

"And you're not going to snitch on friends or relatives. I may not be involved in drug smuggling, but my brother, uncle, aunts, or in-laws may be," says another migrant worker.

Drug dealing has become a normal way of life for many residents of the Texas Valley, so much so that even those not involved say they can't blame those who are. "We have no jobs, we have no money," one migrant worker comments. "This is one fast way of making a lot of money, so people get involved."

According to figures from the U.S. Department of Commerce, the 1990 average per capita income in Starr County was $4,450. The average weekly pay is about $200, the unemployment rate is over 50 percent, and the poverty rate is just as high. And, in a population of over 36,000, almost half—17,509—are migrant workers.

Driving through the county's cactus-dominated landscape, one can see a clear distinction between the people having wealth and those living in poverty. Expensive two-story, brick homes complete with swimming pools, gazebos, and fireplaces—the latter unused because of year-round warm temperatures—stand in the middle of poor neighborhoods. A type of vehicle which indicates the wealth of the owner is the "Choo Choo truck," an American customized pickup with tinted windows, wood panel interiors, chrome, and a powerful sound system.

This is not to say that all owners of beautiful homes and custom-made trucks are drug dealers. Many of these belong to honest, hard-working migrant laborers who have saved their money for years to acquire these possessions. It is the owners of the fine homes built within a few months, or the people who suddenly one day have a beautiful truck parked in their front yard, whom residents say are involved in drug dealings.

Upon returning to their home base after eight months of traveling throughout the U.S., migrant workers gather and talk about the new homes that have been built while they were away.

Chapter 10

LaGrulla Elementary to St. Edward's University

T HE CLASSROOMS IN LaGrulla Elementary School are filled to capacity. Half of the students come from migrant families, which
means they often start school two months after classes begin, and leave
before the academic year is over. Integrating migrant students into the
school system doesn't make their education difficult, school officials
and teachers say. What makes education difficult is inadequate state
funding and a teacher shortage.

Of the 750 students attending LaGrulla Elementary, 320 are from
migrant families. With the high enrollment—100 more than last year—the
school had to open makeshift classrooms, Principal Rose Marie Pena
says. Storage rooms were converted into classrooms last November,
and before that some students were taught in the library and on the
gym stage and floor. Pena says she doesn't know all the reasons why
enrollment keeps increasing. She notices, however, that each year a
larger number of migrant families returns to their home base.

"This year, families that we hadn't seen in two or three years came
back," Pena points out. "From what I understand, these families had
migrated somewhere up north and remained there because there was
work. But this year, they all returned. They're saying there are no
jobs anywhere."

The increase in students has brought with it some problems: first
of all, a space shortage. There are five classrooms each for kinder-
gartners, first-, third-, and fourth-graders; and four rooms each for
second- and fifth-graders. There are about 23 or 24 students per class.

Second, and most importantly, the district has difficulty acquiring
teachers. LaGrulla Elementary School is solving that dilemma by hiring people without teaching certificates to serve as what they call "long-
term substitutes." At LaGrulla Elementary, 3 of the 36 teachers fall
under that category. Pena claims LaGrulla has difficulty hiring teachers
because of low pay and the rural nature of the community.

"Most of the teachers that do work here have to travel 38 miles
a day to and from work," she says.

According to the Texas Education Agency, most of the school districts in the Valley have needed to hire instructors without teaching certificates – called "non-degreed teachers" – in the wake of increased enrollments and teacher shortages. In some districts the substitutes are college graduates, but the ones hired in LaGrulla have high school degrees or General Equivalency Diplomas.

The Texas Education Agency has minimal control over the selection of long-term substitutes and their qualifications. The state of Texas requires only that parents be notified after 30 days that their child is receiving instruction from a non-degreed teacher. Although TEA officials believe having non-degreed teachers in the classroom puts the students at risk of not receiving a good education, Pena says that is not a major concern at her elementary school because of the low number of instructors without teaching degrees.

One way to solve the teacher shortage is through an increase in state funding. But that's doubtful in LaGrulla because the amount of money a school district receives is based on the average daily attendance (ADA).

"The ADA is taken every six weeks, and unfortunately for us, in the spring and fall, enrollment is at its lowest. So we lose out on funding that we would normally be allotted," Pena explains. During the first six weeks of school, most of the migrant families have not returned to Texas.

"They usually don't start arriving until November. And then over half start leaving in March," Pena says. "So during the last six weeks, enrollment is dropped by half."

But even with the lack of qualified teachers, Pena believes students receive a rounded education. She attributes this to the special attention directed at migrant students until they catch up with the rest of the class. Students are tutored or take part in special education, bilingual, or English as a Second Language classes.

"Another reason is because Washington and Oregon have a very good follow-up system. They work very closely with Texas schools," Pena says. "Very good records are kept on each of the migrant students so everybody knows where the child is at [in terms of educational level], where they should be, and what type of special instruction is needed, if any at all."

But, she acknowledges, one of the most important reasons students do so well upon returning to LaGrulla Elementary is because students are not labeled as "migrants."

"Here they are at home, they are with their friends, everyone looks the same, and they all speak the same, primarily Spanish – although in the classrooms they will speak English. So the students don't feel any outside pressure and they're able to better concentrate on their studies," Pena says. "As a matter of fact, when it's time to leave, many students will come into my office to say goodbye – and they're always crying."

For the two youngest children of Raul and Maria Elena, the constant traveling has taken its toll on their education. When the Martinezes arrived in Washington last summer, Billy was 7 and Jimmy, 10. When they began the school year in Boardman, Jimmy put a lot of effort into his class work. Every evening he read his books, did his homework, and studied for tests. He also spoke primarily English while at home, and to his parents.

For younger brother Billy, however, there were difficulties. It was a task to get him to school every morning. Many times Maria Elena physically dragged him out of the apartment screaming, crying, and kicking. At school, he was placed in the federally funded migrant program, which helps migrant children succeed in school and allows them to be mainstreamed with other children. Billy never opened a book once he came home from school, never studied, and was always counting the days left until the weekend. Also, he spoke only Spanish – at home and at school.

Since returning to LaGrulla, there has been a dramatic change in the two. Jimmy has switched to speaking nothing but Spanish – even when I speak to him in English. Rarely does he study at home, claiming he does that at school. However, Jimmy is active in school activities here and will attend school functions, which he never did while in Oregon. For Billy, on the other hand, the only time he speaks in Spanish now is with his father. The rest of his conversations are in English. Every night he works on his homework with help from his mother. Not once has he cried about going to school.

In Oregon, Jimmy came home with A's and B's. Here, he is barely passing. He became a little worried about this when I told him that his grades will be included in his school records in Oregon.

Billy, although he studies now, still does poorly. So every day he puts in extra effort to improve his grades. Billy says he prefers attending classes in Oregon, even though he used to put up a fight every morning in Boardman before going to school. "We didn't have too much homework there," he explains.

Jimmy quickly responds that he likes school in LaGrulla better than in Oregon. "Over there [Oregon], the kids always stared at me when I walked into the classroom because I was the new one. I was the one that always had to try to make friends because they didn't try to make friends with me," he says in Spanish. "All my friends are here, and I don't have to try to meet new people because I already know them."

For migrant children, achieving a high-school education is not always a certainty. However, for those who do graduate from secondary school, there now are programs that help them obtain a college education as well.

College Assistance Migrant Program (CAMP)

Today they are neurologists, attorneys, economists, accountants, and chemists. Yesterday they worked the fields from dawn to dusk, picking fruits and vegetables.

These career professionals have a number of things in common. They all come from migrant families, they hail from the Rio Grande Valley, and they all began their academic careers at St. Edward's University in Austin as participants in the College Assistance Migrant Program (CAMP), a scholarship program offering freshman-year assistance. Throughout the past 20 years, CAMP has allowed students to leave the fields of toil, for fields of dreams.

Since 1972, St. Edward's, a private Catholic college, has actively recruited the sons and daughters of migrant workers, the poorest of Texas's poor. Through CAMP, the university has provided educational opportunities to more than 1,900 migrant students. Each year, 40 students are chosen to participate. CAMP was established largely in response to journalist Edward R. Murrow's early 1960s television documentary "Harvest of Shame." Murrow exposed the bleak reality of migrant life, including the fact that migrant students make up one of the most underrepresented groups in higher education. At the time of Murrow's documentary, only 1 percent of migrant students entering college went on to complete a degree.

St. Edward's responded by developing and hosting the first CAMP program in the nation. Funded by the U.S. Department of Education, the state of Texas, and the university, the program provides participants a combination of financial assistance, and educational and personal services. In addition to tuition, room and board, and books, CAMP students benefit from an array of services geared to first-generation college students, including academic tutoring, career counseling, and health care. Participants receive $12,500 in financial aid, which covers almost all expenses for the first year except $1,500. A majority of students choose to pay the $1,500 balance with a low-interest student loan made available through the university.

"Most students take out the loan, but some will have parents pay the amount in full. If they are academically strong, they may be eligible for other scholarships. But the last thing we want them to do is work," says Robert Gonzalez, St. Edward's CAMP recruiter. "We don't want them to work because we want them to excel in their studies that first year."

Of the 1,900 migrants who have attended St. Edward's, 90 percent have completed the freshman year. Of that number, 58 percent went on to receive college degrees.

"This is very important because it goes to show that given the opportunity and shown the way, these kids do want an education and can get one," Gonzalez explains. "During those last three years of college, the students may take a lesser school load or may take out more loans, receive grants, get on work-study, or they may really excel in academia so that they receive scholarships."

Seven other universities now participate in the program, including Oregon State University, in Corvallis, and Boise State University, in Idaho. Another college in Colorado, and two each in California and Texas also offer CAMP. All of these institutional programs operate in a similar manner; some, however, choose 45 participants each year instead of 40. Migrant students learn about CAMP while in high school when CAMP recruiters, school counselors, and, in many cases, friends who are CAMP participants, encourage students to apply.

"Many of these students are first-generation college attendants. And in many cases the parents are afraid to let them go away on their own, or the parents are afraid it will cost them a lot of money," Gonzalez says. "And in many cases we find students that have a strong belief in family obligation, and going to school means the loss of a wage-earning child." Because of these attitudes, many students will choose to spend summers working with their families in the fields.

"Part of the CAMP financial package includes a monthly allowance of $60, and that's primarily for students to go to a movie or something. But many students will instead send that money home to help their parents and family," Gonzalez points out.

Through CAMP recruiters and the university's Mentor Program, migrant students are urged to get out of the fields and into the classrooms. Gonzalez spends several weeks each semester in the Rio Grande Valley, visiting high schools and explaining the program to students and their families, while reassuring parents that their children will be taken care of while at the university.

"This helps eliminate some of the fear parents have about their child being away from home for the first time," Gonzalez says.

For students who can't be reached at their home base, CAMP representatives at other universities try to seek them out while they travel the country working the fields.

"We spend our time traveling extensively throughout the region trying to reach these students," notes Antonio D. Rodriguez, minority admissions counselor at Boise State University. Rodriguez's region includes the western part of Idaho, the northeastern corner of Oregon including Milton-Freewater, and the southeastern section of Washington, which includes Walla Walla.

"The kids come here and they spend four weeks to four months, and that's when we try to catch them. We also work very closely with the Idaho Migrant Council and the Washington Migrant Council," Rodriguez says.

Since 1984, when the CAMP program opened at Boise State, Rodriguez and other CAMP recruiters have been spreading the word about the program to migrant families throughout California, Washington, Oregon, and Idaho. In the beginning eight years of the Boise State program, CAMP students have come from Washington, Oregon, Texas, Florida, Idaho, New York, California, Michigan, and Nevada.

"If we find a student that is interested in the program but does not live near Boise, we will pay for their transportation to get them here," says Rodriguez.

CAMP recruiters are quick to point out that it does not matter which CAMP program students decide to attend. "The important thing is that they hear about us and that they get a college education," according to Gonzalez.

For many such students, their parents play a central role by encouraging them to attend college. Some children of migrant farm workers say they would have continued working in the fields had their parents not urged them to get an education so they could get out of the migrant cycle.

"My dad used to use reverse psychology on us," recalls 18-year-old Marisela Rodriguez of Alamo, Texas. "He used to say, 'You don't have to go to school if you don't want to. You can work the fields all your life.' I didn't like working in the fields. It was cold, wet, and muddy."

Gustavo Perez, 19, says his parents stressed education because it was something they never had. "They're from Mexico and my dad never went to school one day of his life. My mother only went up to the second grade. In Mexico only the sons of the rich attend school; so for me to attend college is making my parents very proud."

San Antonio attorney Arnulfo Ortiz, 35, says that although his parents pushed education, he always had an inner drive that kept him in the classroom. "School was always easy for me, compared to how we worked in the fields," Ortiz says, laughing.

Ortiz is a 1979 graduate of St. Edward's, and Rodriguez and Perez are current CAMP students at the university. Rodriguez is studying business administration; Perez is studying engineering. Rodriguez, who is one of five children, traveled each year with her parents to Washington, Oregon, and Idaho. "I liked traveling and being on the road," she says. "It was working in the fields that I didn't care for."

Moving in search of work is relatively new to Perez and his older brother and sister. Perez is the son of a ranch hand from Rock Springs, Texas, and it wasn't until five years ago that the family traveled to Iowa, California, and other states in the summer and fall to work on ranches, tending livestock.

"Although we didn't work in the fields or travel throughout the country, we still had to get up at 4 a.m. to work on the ranch before school, and then on weekends as well," Perez says.

Ortiz, the youngest of eight, grew up as a migrant worker. "My brothers and sisters and I would help my mother in the fields because my dad was an amputee, and this was the only way we knew how to make a living," the attorney says. Although born in the border town of Eagle Pass, Texas, Ortiz was reared on the Mexican side, in Piedras Negras. He attended grade school in Mexico, but at age 11 moved with his parents back to Eagle Pass. He had to repeat the fourth, fifth, and sixth grade.

"All this time we were traveling to Minnesota, North Dakota, Idaho, Wisconsin, California, and Oregon," Ortiz says. "It was sad being pulled out of school, but it was an adventure traveling the country. I thought it was fun. My first job was carrying water to people."

Although he remembers the excitement of traveling, he also has vivid memories of the hardships associated with the life of a migrant worker.

"The facilities weren't so good. We lived in tents or shacks and we had to dig holes in the ground for bathrooms," Ortiz says. "We didn't have any money, so we would go to a store and buy bologna and a loaf of bread and eat that for days. As soon as we arrived at a community we had to establish credit because we didn't have any money. I remember one time having to get a loan for gas."

There was also the stigma of being labeled a "migrant" by the other children at school, and the embarrassment of being on welfare and getting free clothes from local agencies, Ortiz recalls. But even with the social and economic barriers, Ortiz put his schooling to good use.

"I served as the interpreter of the family, since a very young age. So I guess I knew all along I was going to do something with my life and not remain a farm worker," Ortiz says.

In 1976, at the age of 19, Ortiz went straight from the fields of South Dakota to St. Edward's through the CAMP program. Three years later, he received a bachelor of arts in history. He worked as a law clerk and legislative assistant during college, and upon graduation was awarded an internship to work for various congressmen in Washington, D. C. Ortiz received his law degree in 1982 and doctor of jurisprudence in 1985, both from Georgetown University. He moved to San Antonio to open a law office in 1985. Currently, Ortiz is seeking the office of Texas state representative.

"I want to work for the older, poorer people," he says. "All my life I saw that they were the ones that were never looked after; yet they're the ones that need the most. Older people shouldn't have to suffer so much."

Rodriguez, as did Ortiz, also went straight from the farm into a college classroom. She hopped a Greyhound bus back to Texas last summer, leaving her family to continue working the potato fields in Hermiston, Oregon.

"I remember school was always hard when I was growing up because we had to work in the fields from 5 a.m. to 3 p.m., then go to school from 6 p.m. to 9 p.m. Then in the summer I had to go to summer school to catch up on what I missed," Rodriguez says. She recalls how some schools in the Northwest—particularly one in Mabton, Washington—didn't have programs for migrant students and how she was not integrated with the other students. "In some schools I was in an office by myself, given a book, and I had to learn it. Some schools didn't care for migrant students," she comments, sounding bitter.

Both Rodriguez and Perez say their parents encouraged them to attend college. "There are some families out there who don't care if their children go to school or not," Rodriguez says. "But then again I don't blame them because the parents' priority is feeding the family, and that's all they're interested in."

In the Perez household, obtaining an education was never a question. "We were not even allowed to think about not going to school. My parents want us to have what they never had."

Both teens say if it weren't for CAMP, they would not be able to attend college. "It's good to know that there are resources available to migrants. All we have to do is take advantage of them," Perez says.

The parents of the two teenage students will continue the migrant cycle until they are too old to continue, or until there is no one left at home. "My parents and younger brothers will go back up north next month, but I'll stay in school," Rodriguez says. "I might go up to work with them in the summer."

Perez's 52-year-old father will continue traveling to California each summer to find work. Both students plan to continue their education until they receive their degrees. Along the way they hope to advise other migrant children that the only way out of the fields is through an education.

Memorial alongside a highway in the South Texas Valley. *U-B Photo*

Roadside market in LaGrulla, Texas (population 1,445). *U-B Photo*

The Martinez home in LaGrulla. *U-B Photo*

"Dia de los Muertos"; Day of the Dead. *U-B Photo*

Six-year project — (l. to r.) Raul Martinez, Jr., Sam Barrera, Jr., Christobal Saenz, and Robert Martinez work on Raul Jr.'s house in Mission, Texas. *U-B Photo*

Two churches—one Catholic, the other Mennonite—are active in LaGrulla. *U-B Photo*

Maria Elena helping Billy with homework. *Isabel Valle*

Bryan Langham of the U.S. Border Patrol on duty in the South Texas Valley. *U-B Photo*

The *Rio Grande. U-B Photo*

Illegal aliens making a run back to the Mexican side of the river. *Isabel Valle*

Gustavo Perez of Rock Springs, Texas, enrolled at St. Edward's University in Austin, Texas, under the College Assistance Migrant Program (CAMP). *U-B Photo*

St. Edward's freshman Marisela Rodriguez of Alamo, Texas, is from a migrant family that annually works in the Pacific Northwest. *U-B Photo*

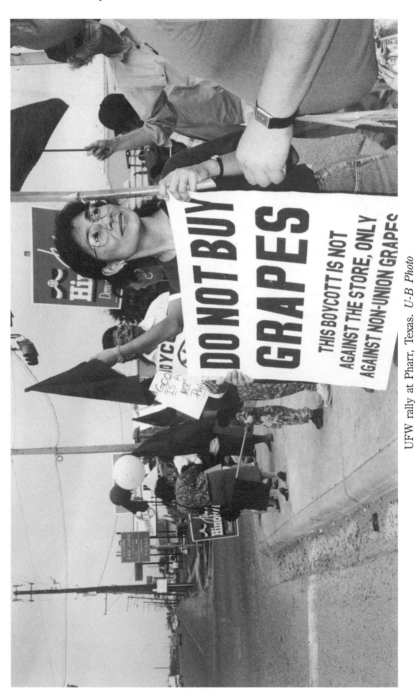

UFW rally at Pharr, Texas. *U-B Photo*

Cesar Chavez (1927-1993). *U-B Photo*

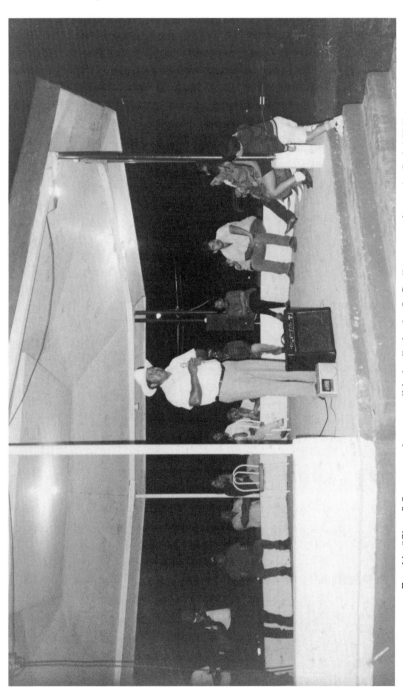

Eusebio "Chevo" Saenz speaks at a political rally in the LaGrulla community park. *Isabel Valle*

Doris Martinez (l.) and Ellen Martinez Herbert. *Isabel Valle*

Maria Elena preparing flour tortillas. *Isabel Valle*

Raul getting the truck ready for the long trip to Pasco, Washington. *Isabel Valle*

Chapter 11

Cheap Labor and the UFW

The boycott is our strength.
— Cesar Chavez

IN 1984, CESAR CHAVEZ called for farm workers and farm worker advocates to boycott the sale of table grapes in an effort to educate consumers about the use of dangerous pesticides on agricultural products. The boycott began as a non-violent means of alerting consumers about the hazards farm workers are exposed to. Today, in various cities and communities in Southern California, and South and Central Texas, farm workers and their supporters continue to picket large chain grocery stores.

Chavez is president of the United Farmworkers of America. [Editor's Note: the following quotes from Cesar Chavez were recorded prior to his death on April 23, 1993, in Yuma, Arizona. He was 66.] UFW officials say that although membership in the union has fluctuated drastically the past three decades, boycotting is one method that still proves effective.

"The boycott is our strength," Chavez said recently during an interview in San Juan, located about 30 miles east of LaGrulla. "We try to get public action to put some force economically so we can get some strength. If you take away customers of a store, they are going to resent it. Boycotting is our best form of winning."

Chavez, who was in San Juan to talk at a United Farmworkers meeting, said the union believes the boycotts inform the public that pesticide exposure is responsible for the high cancer and birth defect rates among farm workers' children. David Martinez, national secretary of the UFW, said the union has documented cases of children being born without fingers, arms, and legs. Their parents worked on farms in California.

"It's scary when children are born with these defects and when children are dying of cancer," Martinez says. "And the parents feel bad because they believe they're bringing the poisons in with them from the fields."

The union maintains the growers benefit financially from the sale of these products, while consumers and farm workers are left to deal with the risks. Martinez claims the union has scored several victories from their boycott: "We've gotten word of a boycott committee as far away as Taiwan."

For a time, the union thought of abandoning boycotts. But UFW officials say they have learned that boycotts are the union's strongest negotiating tool. "When everything fails the boycott does work." Chavez said. "We have to rebuild the structure so that we'll have it. It's going to be a permanent structure of the union."

In addition to grapes, the boycott has expanded to include apples, cherries, lettuce, and tomatoes. One of the major stores targeted in Texas is the H.E.B. grocery store chain. With 200 outlets grossing $2 billion in 1991 in South Texas alone, union officials say this chain store should be sympathetic to their plight, since farm workers comprise more than half of the population in that area.

"We have asked H.E.B. not to promote, advertise, or put California grapes on sale, and still they continue doing so," states Martinez.

H.E.B. replies that they have complied by ensuring the grapes they sell are safe for consumers. Michael De La Garza, H.E.B. vice president of public affairs in San Antonio, says the grocery chain in 1989 began its own pesticide testing program conducted by the Southwest Research Institute in San Antonio: "This began as a result of the growing concern by consumers. We tested for various pesticides that Chavez speaks about."

Store officials met with Chavez in 1990 and supported the boycott by returning $400,000 worth of grapes to California because they did not pass inspection. "That's a big economic loss. So in essence, we were doing in the macro-scale what Chavez is doing in the micro-scale," De La Garza points out.

The grocery chain since then, however, has purchased California grapes and other produce that passed inspection, and will continue to do so under those circumstances. H.E.B. also purchases grapes grown in Chile, which are also tested.

De La Garza says the real issue with the union is survival of the United Farmworkers. Union organizers, however, reject the grocery chain's effort, calling the testing a media ploy because workers in the fields are still exposed to pesticides. They say the boycott is the only way they can get consumers to face up to the issue.

De La Garza believes the boycott will continue because it gets the public's attention. "And we allow them to boycott. We tell store managers to let them pass out their materials and that they're in a safe place when they're picketing, but we also want to make sure that our customers are allowed to go into the store to do their shopping if they so please."

One thing the boycott has not done is to put any type of economic dent in the statewide grocery chain. "As a matter of fact, our sales have had a steady increase of 3 percent to 5 percent each year," De La Garza says.

Cesar Chavez

Cesar Chavez was born March 31, 1927, on his grandfather's small farm near Yuma, Arizona. At the age of 10, he began his life as a migrant farm worker after his father lost a hand and was left disabled. Chavez, along with his parents, brothers, and sisters, joined thousands of other families migrating throughout the Southwest, laboring in row crops, vineyards, and orchards. His formal education ended after the eighth grade when he quit school to help support his family.

Chavez joined the U.S. Navy in 1945. Three years later, he married Helen Fabela, whom he met while working in California vineyards. They settled in the San Jose barrio of "Sal Si Puedes" (Get out if you can).

In 1952, Chavez was working in apricot orchards outside San Jose when he met Fred Ross, an organizer for the Community Service Organization, a barrio-based self-help group then being formed among California's Mexican-Americans. Within several months, Chavez was a full-time organizer with CSO, coordinating voter registration, battling racial discrimination against Mexican-American residents, and forming new CSO chapters across California and Arizona. After failing to convince CSO to commit itself to organizing farm workers, he quit the organization, moved his family to Delano, California, and in 1962 founded the National Farm Workers Association (NFWA).

These were difficult times: "My wife and I worked in the fields seven days a week to support the family. It was during this time that I traveled to dozens of farm communities, slowly building a nucleus of dedicated farm worker members," the farm worker advocate recalled.

In September 1965, Chavez's NFWA, with 1,200 member families, joined the AFL-CIO's Agricultural Workers Organizing Committee in a strike against Delano area table and wine grape growers. For the next five years, Chavez led a successful strike that rallied millions of supporters to the United Farm Workers and formed a national coalition of unions, church groups, students, minorities, and consumers. (The NFWA and AWOC merged in 1966 to form the UFW, and the union affiliated with the AFL-CIO.)

By 1970, the strike convinced most table grape growers to sign contracts with the UFW; however, that year growers in the vegetable industry signed "sweetheart" pacts with the Teamsters Union. In protest of the grower-Teamster agreements, 10,000 farm workers in California's coastal valleys walked out of the fields. In 1973, when the farm workers' table grape contracts came up for renewal, most growers signed with the Teamsters, sparking what Chavez called the largest and most successful farm strike in American history. This event led Chavez to call for a worldwide boycott of grapes, head lettuce, and Gallo wines.

"The boycott forced growers to support then-Governor Jerry Brown's historic 1975 collective bargaining law for farm workers," Chavez said.

The recent international grape boycott, begun in July 1984, was called "The Wrath of Grapes." This theme symbolizes the threats pesticides pose to vineyard workers and consumers.

Chavez resided with his family in La Paz, the union's headquarters at Keene, California, in Kern County's Tehachapi Mountains. Like other UFW officers and staff, he received a $10 weekly stipend plus modest food and living benefits. For the past 30 years, Chavez worked full time to change the working and living conditions of farm workers.

"If you're outraged at conditions, then you can't possibly be free or happy until you devote all your time to changing them and do nothing but that. But you can't change anything if you want to hold on to a good job, a good way of life, and avoid sacrifice. Farm workers will never again be treated like agricultural implements to be used and discarded," Chavez said.

"We have tasted freedom and dignity and will fight to the end before we give it up. We have come too far and we have too much further to go to give up now."

The United Farm Workers' Convocation

About 300 area farm workers gathered in San Juan at the end of February 1992 to hear Chavez speak at the United Farm Workers' 11th Biennial Convocation. Throughout the day-long event, chants of "Viva Chavez," "Viva la causa," "Viva la union," and "Arriba los campesinos" were heard throughout the hall. Chavez told those in attendance that the union has seen an increase in members throughout the past years. The union was at its strongest in 1965-1970, then declined, but started building strength again in 1973.

"We got a lot of pressure but we've been able to overcome all that," Chavez said. "Now we're going to start growing." He noted that in the past 18 months, 4,000 new workers have joined the union. He said the growth was spurred in part by new union efforts, which have been helped by a new recession-driven awareness of the plight of the workers. "People are thinking more today about working people, more than they have in the last 20 years," he said.

The UFW claims to represent hundreds of thousands of farm workers nationwide. But it officially represents only 23,000, all in California, the only state to recognize, with legislation, the union as a bargaining representative. In Texas, there are between 5,000 to 8,000 farm workers in the union, according to leaders.

UFW National Secretary David Martinez said that although there are many farm workers who are not part of the union, they still benefit from the work of the UFW. "The union benefits them because the farmers see what is going on with us and the pull we have so they start treating their workers better to avoid such confrontations with the UFW." Some farm workers say they are reluctant to join the union for fear of retaliation from farmers or because they are fearful they will not get picked for jobs.

During the convocation, resolutions were passed denouncing President George Bush and supporting all Democratic candidates in the 1992 election. According to union leaders, the Reagan administration increased military spending and decreased domestic spending. The poor in this country felt this more than any other group.

"President George Bush has continued the policies of Ronald Reagan and this year we must have a change," said Martinez. "We must make sure that UFW members are registered to vote in November and we must tell the Democratic candidates that we need jobs, jobs, jobs; decent housing, health insurance, and for those who cannot work, humane programs that will help them maintain a decent standard of living," Martinez told a screaming crowd.

"We Need Jobs"

"It's election year and everyone is promising the sky," Raul says while watching a TV report on the New Hampshire primary. "But you can't believe anyone anymore. They say one thing, then they get elected and they do the complete opposite," he complains in Spanish.

It's an election year and like all of America, campaign posters are sprouting up in the South Texas Valley and the tiny community of LaGrulla. Although the hottest election taking place here is that of county commissioner, the U.S. presidential campaign is what interests Raul and Maria Elena the most.

"I think the president—whoever wins—is the one that can help the migrants," Maria Elena says. "But he needs to come down here and talk to the people to see how we live and what we need." She wants the president to see the plight of the migrant worker. "A few years ago I was going to write a letter to President Bush and tell him what we're going through. But some people laughed at me and others thought that it was useless; so I didn't," she says. "But I still think I'm going to. Why not? I'm not afraid."

What Maria Elena wants, as do most migrant workers, is good-paying jobs for the poor people of the Texas Valley. They say that if such jobs were available, they would not have to leave their homes every year to work the fields in the northern states.

"Instead of the president helping us, he's helping other countries. He lets companies build on the other side [of the Mexican border] instead of this side," Maria Elena complains. She was referring to U.S. companies that set up factories just across the border to capitalize on cheap labor. "What President Bush should do is come work with us for a while in the asparagus fields," she says, laughing.

"No. He wouldn't survive because that's hard work and he's not used to hard work," Raul replies.

The Martinezes have not said for whom they will vote in the presidential elections. But in the past they have voted for the Democratic candidate. As for local elections, the Martinezes say they are interested and will attend political rallies. But they do not place much expectation on the candidates.

"What for? They [elected officials] don't do anything for the people anyway," Maria Elena exclaims. "We've lived here all our lives and we haven't seen anything done. Things are still the same as they were years ago. The only one that I really believe is trying to do something for the people is Eusebio Saenz," she says. "Since we've been married I remember he has been trying to do something good for the people."

Saenz is vying for the office of Starr County commissioner, Precinct 3. As Maria Elena's cousin, Saenz has a lot of support from others in the Martinez family as well. Family members and in-laws have said they will vote for him in the Texas primary.

Most migrant workers are registered to vote at home, usually by absentee ballot, since they do not know where they will be on election day. With the Texas primary election set for March 10, one question frequently raised is, "What can candidates do to bring well-paying jobs to the area?"

Congressmen and state lawmakers who have represented South Texas for years say bringing jobs into the area—which has an unemployment rate close to 50 percent—is not as easy as it seems. What they can do, they say, is help create programs that offer other kinds of assistance to people who need well-paying jobs.

"There's a lot of factors that plague the area, one being maquiladoras," explains Texas state representative Rene O. Oliveira, D-Brownsville, who is seeking re-election. "Maquiladoras" are U.S.-owned companies that operate in Mexico near the Texas border so that they can hire cheaper labor. This, migrant workers say, takes away jobs that would normally be given to U.S. citizens. Another problem is the great influx of Mexican nationals who cross the border daily in search of work in the United States. Government officials say these people take away the already-limited number of jobs available to the local residents. "Plus, Texas itself has faced a lot of problems ranging from freezes, droughts, and floods, all of which contribute to the lack of employment," Oliveira says.

Congressional members have tried to help migrant workers by getting legislation passed in Washington, D. C. Kika De La Garza, D-Mission, who has represented the Texas Valley since 1968, helped push through legislation that allows migrant workers who are eligible for food stamps to receive them immediately upon moving to a new location, rather than waiting at least 30 days. Another program, for which De La Garza claims credit, makes people eligible for food stamps and other welfare benefits if they lose their jobs because of natural disasters.

But migrant workers still don't feel that is enough. "These are just handouts that we are getting," county-commission candidate Eusebio Saenz says. "We don't want that anymore. We want jobs."

Many politicians here consider Starr County to be the most poverty stricken in the nation. "Starr County is the poorest county in the United States, and Precinct 3, which is LaGrulla, is the poorest precinct in the county. So, can you imagine how bad we are?" Saenz says. The Texas Employment Commission said unemployment in the county averaged 48 percent last year.

"We also have over 17,000 migrant workers who live in this county. Every year we leave for months to go work up north—and when we return, instead of seeing things moving forward, we find ourselves going backwards," Saenz told about 50 people who gathered recently in a local park to hear him speak.

"With proper administration of federal funds, I believe we can bring in jobs, industries, clinics, and better schools to the area," Saenz adds during an interview. "But the reason we don't see improvements is because those that are in power only think of themselves once they get that power." The incumbent whom Saenz hopes to defeat, Eloy Garza, did not return repeated phone calls from the *Walla Walla Union-Bulletin*.

One consolation for migrant workers is that most say they are treated fairly when they go north to work. "I hear the complaints and I hear the compliments. And there are some farmers who treat the workers very well and that's good because we go so far away, the last thing we need is to be treated unfairly," Saenz says.

Chapter 12

The Trip North

JANUARY. IT'S THE BEGINNING of a new year, winter is upon us, and the migrant workers of South Texas are talking about returning north. The mentality here is, "Although it is only January, it is 'already' January." At the Martinez household, the topic of discussion is who is going to pick asparagus in Pasco this spring. So far, it's only Raul and Robert. Doris and a son-in-law may join the other two as well.

"Doris's job ends in March, and since she just bought a [used] car in November, she needs money to pay it off," Maria Elena says. Currently, Doris is working as a trainee at a lawyer's office in Rio Grande City as part of the federal Job Training Program.

The migrant families talk among themselves about who is going north this year, and who is not. "We're just like the birds: it starts getting cold up north and we can't wait to come home. Then we're home and we can't wait to return," says Maria Elena.

Soon after the Martinezes arrived in Texas, both grandmothers were hospitalized. So Raul's and Maria Elena's days were spent at a nearby hospital. Then came the holidays, and that meant cooking and visiting with friends and family, some of whom came from out of town.

But now that the holidays have passed and the kids are back in school, life has become routine. The first thing Raul does each day is to take Billy and Jimmy to school. Charlie rides the bus. The rest of the day is filled with running errands, such as grocery shopping. Usually the parents are home by 3 p.m., when the children return from school. When there are no errands to run, the couple stays at home and Maria Elena spends the time washing and cleaning while Raul works on his truck, the yard, or the house. Dinner is prepared, and afterward the kitchen is cleaned. Their older sons and daughters often stop by in the evenings; sometimes, Raul and Maria Elena will visit the children at their homes. Maria Elena spends most of the nights helping Billy with his homework.

Some of the older Martinez sons and other migrant workers in the area are trying to find employment, usually seeking jobs as mechanics, in construction, or at the U.S. Border Patrol. But so far little work has been found.

"It's at this time, when we can't find work and it's January and we've already been home two months, that we start thinking about returning up north," Maria Elena says. "We'll just see what happens. March is right around the corner."

The Second Generation's Perspective

During the 17 years that Raul and Maria Elena have been migrant farm workers, the 13 Martinez children grew accustomed to leaving home in the spring to work the fields "up north," and returning home in the fall. As they have grown older and have chosen their own way of living, some have decided to stop migrating, while others continue their parents' traditional lifestyle.

"I like [migrating]. When I was a kid I liked the traveling," states Raul Jr., at 35 the eldest of the Martinez children. In contrast to her older brother, Ellen Martinez Herbert, 24, stopped migrating during her senior year in high school. "It's a part of my life I really resent," she says bitterly. Ellen and her younger sister, Doris Martinez, 20, say the hardest part was leaving friends behind. "We always cried when it was time to go and we would always put up a fight," Doris recalls.

"I didn't like migrating. I didn't like that life. I always wanted something better," Ellen adds. "I remember when I was in high school I kept telling myself that I would make sure I would never marry anyone who migrated. So I never went out with migrants. If there is anything I liked about migrating, I guess it was the traveling. But once we got to our destination it was always work, just from the fields to the house. We never went sight-seeing or anything."

Raul and Maria Elena have worked in the fields since they were married—first in Texas, and then in California, where they lived from 1965 to 1969. They returned in 1970 to Texas, where Raul did farm work near LaGrulla with his brothers and sisters until 1975, by which time the Martinezes had 10 children.

"But he wasn't earning enough. So that is when we, us kids, suggested he go up north. And the first place we went to was Michigan," Raul Jr. says. Other states the family has worked in include Illinois, Minnesota, Washington, and Oregon.

"That's why I keep going up there, because I'm able to make money," Raul Jr. says. That money—about $10,000 in the past three years—has gone toward the construction of his three-bedroom home.

Although some of the Martinez children have found work in Texas, they say they still struggle economically because they are paid the minimum wage of $4.75 an hour or slightly more. Most rely on government assistance. "And that's what I don't want, to be on welfare," Ellen says. "When I was growing up, I used to be embarrassed going to the store and buying with food stamps."

Ellen works full time as a bookkeeper at a local bank. The other children who have jobs in Texas include Emilio, 35, who works full time in an auto mechanic shop; Silvestre, 33, a part-time wood craftsman in Dallas; Esmeralda Martinez Saenz, 32, a full-time tutor at a local school; Hilberto, 30, a self-employed mechanic; Ruth Martinez Barrera, 28, a full-time secretary/scale operator at a local gravel pit; and Doris, 20, a general office clerk for a local attorney. Daniel, 27, and Robert, 19, are unemployed.

All but the five youngest of the Martinez children are married and have their own families; Charlie, Jimmy, and Billy, of course, are still in school. They and Robert are the only children left at home. Doris lives in Rio Grande City, 13 miles west of here. Even though most of them have jobs, migrating is still a part of their lives in one way or another—whether it's because their parents travel from state to state, or because a spouse is gone part of the year. Esmeralda's husband, for example, is a crew leader and migrates yearly. Last year Doris traveled with her family to Pasco to pick asparagus, as did Danny and his wife and children.

"I think if we all had the choice we would all rather stay here. But without jobs, good paying jobs, what can you do?" Raul Jr. says. "If I stay here I won't make any money. And seeing the house, how far we've gotten, it gives me an incentive to continue traveling up north to make money and come home and finish it."

With Iris now five months pregnant, Raul Jr. anticipates migrating a few more years, just to get enough money to finish the house. He expects to complete it in three years and put $15,000 more into it.

"I'd really like to get a steady job so that Abby [their daughter] can stay at one place when she goes to school. I do want the best for my daughter and unborn child," he says. "I don't want her to live like I did. I want her to have a good education."

Ellen, who has a 9-month-old son, says she can see how some people, including her own family, continue migrating each year. "You can make a lot of money in a few months, more than you can here, but the work is hard," she says. "But the most important thing for me is that I want my child to have what I didn't have. I don't want him to grow up the way I did."

And how do they feel about their parents migrating every year? "I'm glad my parents still migrate because I like having them with me," Raul Jr. says.

"I think my parents are too old to continue migrating, but I guess it's OK if they want to because it really makes my father happy when he's working," Ellen says. "But one thing that I'm very grateful for is that Raul Jr. is near them."

Preparations for the Road

It's March, and almost five months have passed since most of the migrant families returned home from working the fields in the Pacific Northwest. Much talk continues about heading north again; farm workers in LaGrulla are buzzing around like busy bees.

"Are you going to go work up north this year?" "What part of the country are you going to?" "Who are you going to work for?" "When are you leaving?" are just a few of the questions heard throughout the South Texas Valley.

To prepare, some families purchase large quantities of soap, toothpaste, laundry detergent, and other personal items that cost much less in Texas than in Washington and Oregon. Some even take out loans from local banks to help them on the road or once they arrive, because they may not see a paycheck for a few weeks. During mid-February, farmers from the Pasco area visited the Texas Valley to recruit workers. Interested migrants wrote down their names and Social Security numbers on a sheet of paper and were told they will be hired.

The Martinez family expects to return to Washington by late March to pick asparagus in the Pasco area. Raul and Robert will be working the fields, as will a nephew, Arnoldo Martinez, 19. "We won't get hired unless we have enough hands, and the least number of workers a farmer will hire is three in a family," Raul explains.

"There are no jobs here anywhere [in Texas]," Raul Jr. said recently. "Everywhere you go people tell us, 'Fill out the application and if anything comes up we'll call you.'" The migrant workers have visited the Texas Employment Commission office seeking employment, and scan the daily newspapers in hopes of finding something. But there are no suitable jobs available. Driving through the small towns that line the Texas-Mexico border, not one "Help Wanted" sign can be seen.

"We're getting nervous. We've been here four or five months and we haven't been able to find work," Fedencia Barrera said recently while visiting the Martinez home. "We are at the point where we have spent all the money we earned [working the fields] and we're not getting anything in." Barrera said all the money she and her family have earned during those years came from farm work.

"We'd like to stay here and work instead of going up north. But when there's no jobs, you have to pick up and go," Barrera said. "The last thing we want to do is live off welfare." Two of Barrera's children are married to two of the Martinez children.

Even some Martinez family members say they are tired of heading north each spring. "But at least up there we know we will make some money," Maria Elena says. "Down here what do we do?"

"And I like it," says Raul. "I don't think there is anything wrong with working in the fields. It's good, hard, honest work."

During the past few weeks, Raul has been preparing his 1989 Ford truck, making sure it is in good operating condition for the road. He has often considered buying a newer truck, but the least expensive one he found cost about $5,000. While that would be considered a good deal for a newer used truck in the Northwest, Raul considers the amount to be too much. In South Texas, it's not unusual for people strapped for cash to unload vehicles for a fraction of what they are worth.

Maria Elena talks about looking forward to visiting with friends she has made during the many years of traveling in Washington and Oregon. Even Jimmy and Billy say they look forward to returning. "We have fun up there. At least up there we can go to a park or to the river. Here [in LaGrulla] there is nothing to do," Jimmy comments.

The only one not excited about leaving Texas is Charlie, who will turn 16 in June. "Don't even talk to me about that place," he says. "This is my hometown and I like it here. I miss it when I am away."

As their days in Texas draw to an end, all eyes and ears are on the weather forecast. After leaving the mid-80-degree temperatures of South Texas, they possibly will be traveling in snow storms in Utah and southern Idaho, before reaching the Columbia Basin and its springtime weather. Maria Elena is responsible for packing clothes, utensils, and personal items that will be carried with them to Washington. This year as in the past, her daughters assist in packing.

Most migrant workers return to Washington in April, just before the usual beginning of the asparagus season. However, this year, Raul, Maria Elena, and five of their children leave March 17, arriving in Boardman on the 20th. They leave early because Raul Jr. was told by his employer in Boardman to return as soon as possible.

"It's always better to travel with someone else and not alone because you never know what may happen on the road," Raul says. "Besides, Junior knows everything about cars and if something should happen to any of the cars he can repair it," Maria Elena adds.

The Arrival

"Oh it's so good to be back." "It feels like we didn't even leave." These are the remarks from members of the Martinez family upon their arrival.

"This is like our home away from home," Maria Elena says shortly after they arrive in Boardman. "Seeing my friends from here is like seeing members of my own family."

The family has settled into their two-bedroom mobile home in the Lake View Agri-Park Labor Camp located on the outskirts of Pasco. The family spent the first two nights in Boardman with Raul Jr., before they moved into the trailer park in Pasco.

The trip from Texas to Washington went smoothly compared to the snow, sleet, rain, and high winds encountered last October during the trip home to La Grulla. This time, sunshine and mild temperatures cut travel time to three days. Outside of Albuquerque, New Mexico, the three-car caravan encountered heavy snow, but it only lasted about 30 minutes. Only once did the mini-caravan have to pull over to the side of the road so Raul could check under the hood of his truck. He had heard rattling, but saw no problems so they continued on without further mishap. The small caravan of cars would start out about 5 a.m. and drive until 9 p.m., covering over 700 miles per day.

During the first two days in Boardman, Raul contacted former employers so he would have work after the asparagus harvest. He was told he would have his old jobs back this summer. Meanwhile, Maria Elena spent time visiting with Boardman residents who have become close friends of the family. She presented each friend with a small gift that she had brought with her from Texas.

The family wanted to settle into its temporary home as soon as possible, so Raul and Maria Elena spoke with the managers of the labor camp in Pasco to see if they could move into the park early. (The migrant camp is closed until late March or early April.) The park managers decided to let the family in early, since they had already arrived and had no place to stay. The first day in Pasco was spent unloading, unpacking, cleaning the trailer, getting to know the area, and purchasing food and other necessary items. There was also the task of getting the three youngest boys enrolled in school.

About 75 percent of the trailers in the labor camp are deserted, since migrant families have not started arriving yet. But the camp is expected to be filled to capacity within the next two weeks. And most who are scheduled to travel to Pasco to work in the asparagus fields are friends of the Martinez family from LaGrulla or South Texas.

This year, Raul says he needs money to support the youngest members of his family and he wants to purchase a new truck. Robert was unable to find work in Texas, so he has to returned to the Northwest. Last year he didn't come in order to graduate from high school. Arnoldo, who has never worked the fields before, said he decided to travel north this year with his aunt, uncle, and cousins to get money to buy a car so he can go to college next fall. "I wasn't going to do anything this summer, absolutely nothing. I was just going to stay at home." But Arnoldo finally "decided to come up here to work so I can buy my own car." He adds, "But this is my first and last time I am going to work the fields." Charlie will not be working the fields until possibly this summer, when school is out.

The Martinez children who have remained in Texas hope that this is the last year their parents will travel north to work the fields. They say their parents should no longer continue the migrant life, since Raul is receiving Social Security and there are only four children left at home. Raul receives nearly $500 a month in Social Security, and they have lived off of it while in Texas. The money Raul saved from working the fields last year, about $5,000, bought clothes for the family and a washing machine. With the little that is left, plus what he earns this year, he plans to purchase a new truck and a clothes dryer.

Charlie says, "I'm going to leave this place before my parents do. I am going to go home by bus this summer like I did last year. And then that's it, I'm not coming back anymore," he says speaking to himself.

He exclaims he does not want to attend high school in Pasco until his friends from Texas arrive. He says he is embarrassed to walk into a classroom alone, not knowing anyone there. The two younger boys also do not want to start school, but only because they wish to spend the days with Robert and Arnoldo. They consider this a mini-vacation and it is difficult for them to understand that they must complete their school year in Pasco.

"The boys have already missed one week of school with the traveling and all, I really need to get them enrolled as soon as possible," Maria Elena says.

Robert was not eager to leave his friends and family behind in Texas. When he first arrived at the trailer park, he walked into the mobile home, sat on the sofa, and, as he watched the rest of the family unload the truck, he said half jokingly, "I'm not going to stay here. I only came for the ride."

Field work is expected to start within the next few days, meanwhile Robert and Arnoldo are trying to enjoy their free time as much as possible. Once the work begins, the two will have to start their days at 4 a.m. and get to bed by 8 p.m. Raul and Maria Elena have spent their time going into "el pueblo" each day to supply the house. Once the field work begins, Raul will be taking the truck to work and Maria Elena will be left without transportation.

"Once [all the other migrant workers] start arriving and the work begins, then we will really feel like we're at home. We do a lot of visiting after work and on weekends. It's just like being in LaGrulla," Maria Elena says.

Part III
March-June

Chapter 13
Pasco Asparagus Harvest

IN ABOUT A WEEK'S TIME, the almost-deserted labor camp on the outskirts of Pasco has begun to come to life, as truckloads of families arrive to work in the asparagus fields. Most of the workers are U.S. citizens. Some of the migrants, including the Martinez family, had jobs and housing lined up before arriving. Some get jobs based on references from friends, family members, and even former employers. These farm workers are usually bilingual and may have high school degrees.

Joining these migrants is another type of migrant worker, traveling from as far away as southern Mexico or Central America. Some of these people arrive in the Pacific Northwest hungry and without a cent. They haven't eaten in days, and come with only the clothes on their backs and a deep desire to find work—any work. In Walla Walla, a number of people from the southern Mexican state of Oaxaca have been arriving since early March. They usually enter the United States through California and continue heading north, working in fields along the way.

"We come up here because back home we hear this is a good place to find work," one migrant worker says in Spanish. He and his companions ask not to be identified. "We are told there is work here, the pay is good, and that there are services available for field workers."

According to the Washington State Department of Employment Security, farm workers picking onions last year in Walla Walla County and statewide earned $4.50 an hour on average. Asparagus cutters received $4.25 an hour. Apple harvesters were paid $4.31 an hour in Walla Walla County, and $4.69 an hour statewide.

The six Oaxacans say they have not been able to find work since they arrived a month ago. They came early so they could find housing. "We've worked in fields in California, here in Washington, and in Oregon, and sometimes farmers provide us with housing," one of them comments. "But in this case we do not know a farmer here that will provide us with housing, so we have to look for one ourselves. We know we have to come early to get some place to live or we won't find anything," he adds.

"People arriving later have to sleep in their cars," another man says as his companions listen. It is a lazy Sunday afternoon; the men are outside their apartment complex enjoying music. These farm workers have found small apartments on Eagan Street, on the west side of Walla Walla. As many as four people live in a one-bedroom unit. Rent is $120 to $300 a month, plus electricity.

Gary Meister, director of the Christian Aid Center in Walla Walla, says that when migrants arrive they add to the already existing problem of homeless people. His center, which is privately funded, houses migrants and others needing a place to stay. "Last year we spent $2,000 in a week to put in new showers and beds to accommodate the workers that were coming in," Meister says.

Because of crop damage in California, a large influx of migrant workers traveled to Walla Walla last year to work the onion and asparagus crops. "The cycle of homeless goes down during the winter months," when migrants return to their homes, he points out. "But this year it didn't do that, primarily because today we have a problem with local homeless" people.

To help reduce problems of overcrowding, Meister is asking local churches to take in a few families. Churches are requested to either house families in their buildings, since kitchens are available, or ask parishioners to take migrant families into their homes.

Meister's center will provide housing to migrants as long as they need it, so they can have a warm place to sleep and three meals a day. "As long as people are making an honest effort to work, then they can stay here," Meister says. "I know that migrants are some of the hardest working people around, and I don't have any problems with them staying here. I know of a lot of local Realtors that will purposely not rent to blacks or Hispanics, and I just think that is a downright shame because some of those people are really hard working and are looking to make an honest living."

Migrant workers are already arriving at his shelter, but none as yet have found the need to stay long-term. "We had a group in here of about 20 people a couple of weeks ago, but they just spent the night before moving on to Dayton. Another group came in later, but just for gas," he points out.

Little LaGrulla

Migrants living here say they have never dubbed the Lake View Mobile Home Park by any other name than "el parque" (the park), but

I think "Little Texas" or, better yet, "Little LaGrulla" is much more descriptive. Almost everyone here is from that community.

We were the first to arrive in the camp and as other families come in, the Martinezes are always the first to greet the new arrivals. Maria Elena and Raul will brew a fresh pot of coffee and take it to the families as they arrive. It's been a month since we've been here and all 250 trailers are filled. It's almost as if we never left Texas. With just the visit of one person to our trailer we are immediately informed of who's getting married back home, who's having a baby, who bought a new car, who has died, who's sick, and on and on.

The people in the labor camp are a very tight group. There is a lot of sharing going on. If you need a baby-sitter, all you have to do is knock on a few trailer doors and soon you'll have a baby-sitter. There is a lot of sharing of food from one trailer to another. People share ironing boards and irons, vacuum cleaners, brooms, and mops. Even the kids share their clothes. If one family has a cable TV hook-up, you can be sure there will be a large gathering of people at the trailer every evening. If one family has a telephone, that number is distributed to the other nearby families as the "emergency" number, in case family members back home need to get in touch with someone immediately.

The trailer camp itself has a warm feeling to it. The camp always begins stirring at the same time each morning, usually around 5 a.m. In the evening, between 9 p.m. and 10 p.m., lights are starting to be turned off and all becomes quiet and still. During the late afternoon and early evening you can see male teenagers playing a game of basketball as female teenagers walk around the camp. The men in their 20s and 30s are usually gathered in a group sitting on the lawn listening to music, drinking beer, or washing and fixing their trucks and cars. Children run all over the camp playing. The women are cooking dinner, and after supper has been eaten and the kitchen cleaned, they too will go visiting with their neighbors.

This is the first time I have lived in a labor camp and I don't find it any different than living in a friendly apartment complex. We have communal laundry facilities and public telephones, and there is even a woman who has set up the front room of her trailer as a miniature candy store, where she sells Mexican candy to the camp children.

The migrants don't talk about being homesick, and I can now understand why: they are at home. But come June, when the asparagus harvest is over and people start packing their belongings to return home or to move on in search of other jobs, then the homesickness sets in. In their new locations, their neighbor may not be from LaGrulla, may not even be from Texas, may not even be Hispanic. That's when they start feeling like they are far from home, and start looking forward to the day when they can return to what they're familiar with.

The Harvest

The asparagus harvest began April 1 this year, earlier than usual because of the mild winter and an early spring. Asparagus is the first crop of the year, according to the Washington Asparagus Commission, and normally provides jobs for as many as 10,000 workers. Although some asparagus is being harvested early, hundreds of workers have arrived at the labor camps and are waiting for work in the fields. Despite the early start, asparagus cutters have been able to work only a few hours each day. The first day they were in the fields from 6 a.m. to 1 p.m.; the next four days they worked from 6 a.m. to only 9 or 10 a.m.

"We're getting less hours because there is not too much work yet, and there are a lot of people out in the fields," Robert says. Field work is limited because temperatures dropped and rains moved into the area.

"We had a decent run for the first couple of days because of the warm temperatures," says Mike Harker, administrator of the Washington Asparagus Commission, based in Kennewick. "The first of April is rather early for asparagus harvesting, and I think Mother Nature tricked us a bit with the warm weather, but the kind of weather we've had lately is typical for this time of year." Ideal growing weather is 80-degree days and 45-degree nights.

When the season gets into full swing, farmers in Washington can harvest up to 3 million pounds in a day, according to Washington Asparagus Commission officials. The harvest traditionally lasts until mid-June, depending on the weather. Usually, asparagus returns about $45 million annually to farmers and is worth another $55 million to the economy when packing and processing costs are added, Harker explains.

California asparagus, which competes with Washington's, recently was selling in Tri-Cities supermarkets for about $1.89 a pound. When the local asparagus comes on the market, that price may drop to about $1 a pound in the Tri-Cities. As the season goes on, the price may go below $1. In Walla Walla, supermarkets were selling California fresh-cut asparagus for 79 cents to 99 cents a pound. Some had already sold locally grown asparagus. Farmers who sell directly to the public often sell their produce for between 50 cents to 70 cents a pound, Harker says.

According to the Asparagus Commission, Washington and California are about equal in asparagus production. Together they produce nearly 80 percent of the nation's output. Roughly 30 percent of Washington's 29,000 acres of asparagus is grown for the fresh market. The rest is canned or frozen at processing plants.

Skilled Laborers

Asparagus cutting, considered one of the most grueling forms of manual labor, requires a certain technique to be done properly.

"Asparagus cutting is a skilled labor, by all means," notes Harker. "Farmers usually seek out cutters that have previously worked the harvest, because the asparagus has to be cut a certain length, placed in the field boxes in a certain manner, and cutters have to distinguish between usable asparagus and non-usable asparagus."

During peak work periods, cutters normally are bent over for about six hours a day with field boxes carried over their shoulders. They cut the asparagus at a minimum of 6½ inches with a slice diagonal to the ground.

"I never thought work could be so hard," Arnoldo said as he slowly climbed into bed at 7 p.m. Having never been in the fields before, he had worked seven hours on the first day of this year's harvest.

Asparagus harvest workers say that although this is one of the hardest jobs, one can earn a lot of money.

"You can earn as much as $8,000 to $10,000 during a season, if the harvest is good and if you work real hard," says Fendencia Barrera. "If you have a lot of hands working in one family, you can really make a lot of money." She, with her husband, two sons, and a daughter-in-law, will be cutting asparagus. Last year, Raul and Maria Elena earned about $4,000. They say they didn't do as well as expected. The previous year they earned a little over $8,000.

Doing piece work, "a good cutter can make as much as $8 to $10 an hour," Harker says.

Some migrant workers come here intending only to cut asparagus, then return to Texas. Raul, however, stays in the Northwest and will continue working the fields for at least three more years, or until he feels he can no longer do manual labor.

This particular manual labor—cutting asparagus—requires a rigorous schedule as well as skill.

Life during the Harvest

It's 4 a.m. when country-western music erupts from a radio-alarm clock located in the tiny living room of the trailer home. For five minutes, the music rocks the trailer before one of the three boys sleeping in the living room decides to get up and turn it off. "Surely by now the other six people that live in the two-bedroom trailer have been awakened from their deep sleep," he thinks.

Maria Elena gets out of bed, puts on a housecoat, and sleepily makes her way down a dark hall and through the living room into the kitchen. The light switch is turned on, and pots and pans rattle. She must prepare a hearty breakfast—and lunch—for her son and husband who will be working the asparagus fields that day. Breakfast usually consists of flour tortilla tacos of eggs and beans and a pot of coffee. For lunch, the men will take with them flour tortilla tacos of ground beef, potatoes, and rice and a thermos of Kool-Aid. Water is also carried in a spare thermos.

It's 4:30 a.m. when Maria Elena calls for her 19-year-old son to wake up. "Robert, it's time for you to get up," she tells him. "Go wake up your father."

After a few seconds of moaning and laying in bed, Robert drags himself into the bathroom to wash up. Within minutes he walks out of the bedroom in his working clothes—an old pair of jeans, shirt, pullover sweater, tennis shoes, and a cap.

"Dad, it's time to get up. Time to go to work," he tells his father. Raul quickly hops out of bed and into the bathroom.

Back in the kitchen, Maria Elena is packing their lunch while Robert is eating. "Don't eat too much because then you might get sick while you're bending over cutting asparagus," Raul warns his son.

It's almost 5 a.m., and still dark and chilly outside. As they make their way out the door, vehicle headlights can be seen moving about the labor camp as other migrant workers leave for work. The men get into their truck, joining the rest of the cars and trucks slowly emptying out of the labor camp.

Maria Elena begins cleaning the dishes and then quickly prepares breakfast for Charlie who will be getting up soon to go to school. She tries to remain as quiet as possible so as not to wake Charlie and Jimmy, who are laying a few feet away from her. Thirty minutes later the kitchen is clean, and Charlie's breakfast is warming on the stove. Maria Elena returns to her bedroom to try to get some rest. However, she finds that difficult since she needs to keep an eye on the clock to make sure Charlie does not oversleep. At 6 a.m. Charlie is awake. Usually there is no trouble getting him out of bed. He quickly races to the bathroom, washes, dresses, and proceeds to the kitchen to eat. At about 6:45 a.m. there is a knock on the trailer door. It's one of Charlie's friends. The two boys always accompany each other to the bus stop down the street.

The trailer remains quiet for a while, until it's time to wake up the two youngest boys for school. This is usually a task for Maria Elena, so at 7:30 a.m. she gets out of bed again and goes directly to the living room where she turns on the television. She finds a channel that is airing cartoons, and tells Billy to hurry and get dressed for school so he can have time to watch television and eat before the bus comes. Jimmy usually jumps at the offer.

Billy sleeps with his parents in their bedroom, which is at the end of the trailer. Many times Maria Elena has to physically pull him out of bed and drag him to the bathroom. It takes about an hour for the boys to dress, eat, and watch a little television before the bus comes to pick them up.

At 8:30 a.m. the trailer is quiet with everyone out to either work or school. The kitchen must be cleaned again and the beds must be made. Since Jimmy sleeps on the floor on top of layers and layers of blankets, they all must be folded and put away. A tiny two-bedroom trailer with seven people living in it can get untidy rather quickly, so every day it must be cleaned. It's usually 11 a.m. or so when the cleaning is completed. Maria Elena may fill the next two hours with doing the laundry, ironing, going to the grocery store, running errands, or sometimes baby sitting.

At about 1 or 2 p.m., workers start returning home from the fields. Raul and Robert enter the trailer looking tired and hot, but still very energetic.

"We picked 19 boxes today"; "There was lot of asparagus out there"; "Boy, was it hot," are some of the comments that are heard every day. They take quick showers, change clothes, and get a bite to eat. Sometimes, Maria Elena has a warm meal waiting for them. Robert will usually settle in for a nap on the bottom bunk set up in the living room, but Raul will normally go into town on errands or shop for clothes for the kids.

At 3 p.m. the door swings open. Billy and Jimmy are home. "I'm hungry, what can I eat?"; "What's on television?" Their mother gives them a snack and they sit in front of the TV. The noise wakes up Robert so he gets out of bed. An hour later Charlie arrives from school and the same comments can be heard from him. Between then and dinner, the boys visit their friends in the trailer park. Raul will also make house visits.

Members of the Martinez family eat dinner at different times, usually between 5 p.m. and 7 p.m. After dinner, Raul will go outside to wash his truck, while the boys either stay inside watching television or go outside to visit with friends. Maria Elena will quickly clean the kitchen so she too can visit with neighbors.

By 9 p.m. Robert and Raul are back and preparing for bed. Their working clothes must be ready for the next day, and it's time to turn off the television. A little resistance is put up by the younger boys, but by 10 p.m. all lights in the trailer are turned off and everyone goes to sleep.

The next day it starts all over again.

How It All Started: Green Giant's Asparagus Fields

Hearing it told, one would think Texas migrant workers were the ones who kept Green Giant in operation for over 20 years. As the story goes, when Green Giant first opened in Dayton in 1942, American Indians were recruited to work the fields—but they quit because they considered the work too hard. At that time, Green Giant was harvesting and processing peas and corn.

Next, Green Giant employers flew to Puerto Rico to pick up interested islanders. They only lasted one harvest season, quitting when they found the food was not cooked to their liking; rice and chicken were prepared "a la Mexicana." Then the Washington State Department of Labor and Industries bused in homeless and unemployed people from Seattle to work the fields. That too was short-lived. Green Giant officials spent more time and money busing people back to Seattle than busing them to the job.

But in 1965, Ruben Solis, a life-long resident of LaGrulla, told company officials that he could get complete families to work for Green Giant. By this time Green Giant began leasing land near Pasco to asparagus growers, and it also added asparagus to the crops being raised at Dayton. (In 1987, the company stopped growing its own vegetables and began purchasing the raw product directly from growers.)

"Up until that time, 1965, we were only hiring singles. We used to pay for 14 or 15 Greyhound buses to bring the single men and a few women up to Pasco and Dayton from Eagle Pass, Texas," says Ricardo Guardado, Green Giant's human resources supervisor in Pasco. "But then Ruben told us that he had families that could do the work, and he wanted Green Giant to give him a chance."

Solis, whom Green Giant officials now refer to as "the Godfather," was given a chance. He brought a few families from LaGrulla, and they were given a certain number of acres to clear near Pasco.

"The story goes that when Green Giant officials went out into the fields one afternoon to see how the families were doing, they found the fields empty. The officials were ready to go back to Ruben and say, 'See, we told you having families out there wouldn't work.' But instead what happened was that the fields were empty because the work was already completed," Guardado says, giving a hearty laugh. That was in 1965, and from then until 1987, families from LaGrulla, as well as single people from Eagle Pass, were hired by Green Giant to work the fields it leased.

"We started developing relations with the leaders in those communities, and that's why they kept coming up here to work. But Ruben Solis and George San Miguel, from Eagle Pass, were the ones that opened the doors for us," Guardado says.

San Miguel, 70, no longer travels to this part of the country, but remains an adviser for Green Giant when it is recruiting workers from Texas. Solis died in LaGrulla in 1984. Guardado, who has been with the company for 12 years, recalls how as many as 600 single workers came from Eagle Pass and 800 families from LaGrulla.

"We're told we used to empty out LaGrulla," he says of the tiny community, which now has 1,445 residents. Since entire families were mobilized to come to the Pacific Northwest each year to work the fields, the issue of housing had to be addressed.

"Green Giant believed in providing for the worker, so that's when we started renting trailers from the trailer parks for families to live in. We allotted 4.4 adults per trailer; sometimes it was more and sometimes it was less. And we paid up to $700 a month per trailer. Sometimes we rented as many as 400 trailers," Guardado says.

He believes that the major factor that drew so many families to the area was Green Giant's decision to provide free housing. "Plus, because of the amount of work that there was, we used to tell them that a family of up to four workers would earn a minimum of $4,000 for 65 days of work, the company would pay each worker $75 for their trip up here, and we provided them with medical and life insurance and workers compensation. This insurance began once they left their homes—even during the days of traveling they were considered as our employees," Guardado explains.

People from LaGrulla took advantage of the opportunities given them by Green Giant. As a result, two generations have kept alive the tradition of traveling to the Northwest to work. Today, they are hired by asparagus farmers, but Green Giant still employs them for its processing and grading plants.

"However, Green Giant never stopped associating with the worker. For example, we advise the grower how to treat the workers. And when [the farmer] goes down to Texas at the end of winter to recruit workers, we travel along with them and hold seminars with the growers and workers," Guardado explains. "We tell the grower that it's very important for them to travel to Texas and meet his employee in his hometown. That puts the farmer and worker on the same level, both need each other, and they work better together."

Green Giant also employs people from LaGrulla to work as graders in Pasco's centralized receiving station. A grader is someone who receives, trims, and weighs samples of asparagus spears according to specification. The samples provide the company with information about the grower and the cutter. Cutters are then paid based on that information. "This is very important because we want the worker to know that they are being graded not by a Green Giant official, but by their own sisters, wives, mother, family member," he says.

Guardado also travels to Green Giant plants in Idaho, North Carolina, Wisconsin, and Minnesota to assist in applying the same system Green Giant has developed here in Pasco and Dayton. "The first thing I ask plant officials is if they have money because if they don't, they may as well forget it."

"The first thing anybody has to do if they want to bring in workers is provide housing. You don't find too many families that will move unless housing is provided. And if you're going to bring in families, then you have to start talking about education, day care, preschool, medical attention. There is just a list of things you have to think about when you want to move families from one community to another," says Guardado.

He adds that many communities elsewhere in the nation do not provide anywhere near the level of assistance for farm workers as do some communities in the Pacific Northwest. But as more and more farm workers migrate to those locations year after year, Guardado hopes these communities too will start opening their doors to them.

Crew Leaders

Hiring good crew leaders is an important way to provide for the needs of farm workers. When people speak of crew leaders, they think of someone who only recruits people to work the fields in various parts of the country. In Spanish they are referred to as "tronquistas" or "coyotes," the latter being a derogatory term. The literal translation of "tronquista" is "trucker," but migrant workers use the term to refer to someone who hires workers to harvest crops. The term "coyote" often indicates a swindler who charges people a fee to bring them to the northern states to work—but when they arrive, there is no work and people are left there with no way of returning home.

Some crew leaders are outstanding people in their communities who are looked up to and admired. "A crew leader is a real leader in the community," Guardado points out. "He has to have money in the bank because a lot of times he has to co-sign loans. And many times he serves as an adviser."

When migrant workers from Texas prepare for their long journey to the Pacific Northwest, they can be heard asking crew leaders such questions as "How's the temperature up there?"; "Are the roads cleared enough to travel them?"; "Do you know if there's going to be a big crop this year?"; and, "Will housing be prepared for us when we get there?" They also often ask favors of their crew leaders, the most common of which is arranging for financial loans.

For the past 2½ decades, Juan Antonio Garcia, of LaGrulla, has been a crew leader. He says he has brought "hundreds and hundreds" of people to the Northwest to work the fields. Garcia earlier had been employed with an airplane parts company in northern Texas. Because he had worked the fields since childhood and was accustomed to hard labor, Garcia decided to become a crew leader.

"I always liked working the fields," he says. "I never liked being indoors."

Garcia's first job as a crew leader took him to Grandview for two years, then to Walla Walla for another two. In 1972 he traveled to Pasco and has been returning there ever since.

"During those first years as crew leader I remember co-signing a lot of bank loans and lending money to people," Garcia reminisced. "In those days, times were hard if you didn't have a job because there was no such thing as food stamps or unemployment [compensation for migrant workers]. People needed money for homes, to live off of while they weren't working, and to get them over here to work. We used to lend people amounts of $200 to $700." Sometimes Garcia loaned money out of his own pocket; other times, he co-signed bank loans.

"When I would lend out my own money I would ask people to pay me back a little at a time from their paychecks. But there were times I never got paid back at all. After a while I stopped noticing how much money I loaned out."

Besides assisting people with financial problems, Garcia has helped them make decisions on purchasing vehicles, on obtaining an education for their children, and on who to go to for medical attention.

He and other crew leaders also have the responsibility of hiring field workers. "That was never really hard back then because the people of LaGrulla had always been field workers," says the 56-year-old Garcia. In those days families from that tiny community traveled throughout Texas, picking cotton and citrus fruits. Garcia says he normally brought about 80 workers with him. They ranged in age from 14 to 74. This year Garcia hired 78 workers from the South Texas Valley to cut asparagus.

"Now it's getting harder to get workers because people that came up here as children went on to get a good education and are now working professionals. Thinking back, people that today are working as bankers, professors, doctors, and lawyers all started off with me working in the fields," he proclaims proudly, as if he were talking about his own children.

Garcia says he does not consider the people he hires today to be true asparagus cutters because they've only been doing it five or six years. "But still there are some families that have stayed with me all along," he points out. That includes the Martinezes, who have been traveling with Garcia since 1981.

Garcia begins each day at 5 a.m., walking behind his workers in the fields and watching how the asparagus is cut. He stays out there until the last cutter has completed his work, which may be 3 p.m. If the asparagus is not cut to specification, the farmer confronts the crew leader.

The workers "get paid by the amount of usable pounds that they cut. So if they want to get paid well they have to know how to cut the asparagus. For those that are new, I walk alongside of them as they are cutting and I show them how to cut. I'll stay with them for a couple of days to make sure they are doing it right. But the majority of the people that work with me know how to cut, so I don't have to keep a real close eye on them."

Crew leaders are paid in various ways, depending on the contract they have with the farm owner or operator. Some receive a percentage of the usable pounds each worker cuts; others may earn a certain amount per hour per worker—for example, 10 cents an hour for every worker—and others may receive hourly wages.

One of the major problems crew leaders face is the possibility of workers returning to Texas before harvest has been completed. Christobal Saenz, Raul and Maria Elena's son-in-law, is a crew leader in Othello. He says that when a worker leaves, it is the crew leader's responsibility to find a replacement immediately.

"Each worker is given a certain amount of acres. The ones that have experience, of course, get more acres and the others get less," Saenz explains. "When someone leaves, I either have to hire someone else or I have to add more acres to one of my better workers. Sometimes that can be a problem, because everyone is tired as it is. To add more acres to their workload can be very hard." But Saenz and Garcia note that most of their workers stay on until the harvest is completed.

Garcia says he enjoys his work and has become close to the families who have worked for him. He has served as godfather to their children, as groomsman in numerous weddings, and even as a pallbearer. He has no expectation as to when he will retire.

"I hope to continue doing this for as many years as I can," Garcia says. "But I'll always say that when the farmer that I work for no longer plants asparagus, then that is the day I will no longer come up here."

Chapter 14

Is Education Enough?

BEING PULLED OUT OF schools twice a year and placed in new schools in new locations was not a problem with the Martinez children when they were younger. But when they started getting older and noticing the environment around them, that's when the difficulties started arising.

In one school year, Charlie, Jimmy, and Billy are placed in three different schools in three different states. They usually begin the school year in Oregon, then are transferred to Texas in the fall, and by spring they are enrolled in Washington. The most difficult hurdle they encounter is trying to be accepted and make friends.

Billy never has difficulties when he's being pulled out of school. (He likes the idea of not having to go to school.) But he also is quick to adjust to new schools.

"As long as I have friends to play with at school, it really doesn't matter where I am," he'll say. "But I do like Texas better because that is where I have the most friends."

For Jimmy, things are a little harder. As he gets older it starts getting more difficult for him to say good-bye to his friends. He starts building a bond with some of his "buddies" in any school that he is at, then a few months later he has to break that bond. "It's hard saying good-bye to friends," he says. But like his little brother, he too makes friends easily.

The one who has the most difficulty is Charlie. As children, it's easy to get along with others. Children do not notice color or race. To them, all that matters is that they have someone to play with. But as they start getting older, they begin to notice differences, and labels start getting in the way. That is the difficult part for Charlie. He has two labels attached to him—"migrant" and "Hispanic." Charlie missed the first week and a half of school when we first arrived in Pasco because he did not want to go to the high school without his friends. (They were not scheduled to arrive until two weeks later.) His parents enrolled him in school and kept after him to attend, but Charlie would not budge.

"I'm not going to go alone. I'm not going to know what classroom to go to, who my teachers are. I'm going to be there all lost. I'm not going to school until the others arrive," he repeated nightly during the first two weeks.

Soon his friends did arrive. On the night before they were preparing to go to school, he and four of his friends sat outside the trailer discussing their new school.

"Well, tomorrow we'll stick together and if anybody says anything to us, we just won't pay any attention to them," one of them said. They all agreed that they would support one another in school. Later that night, Charlie walked into the trailer and was preparing his clothes for the next day. He had a different walk and look about him. The expression on his face and his movement said, "Yeah, I'm tough and no one can mess with me." It was at that point that I realized the reason for his change. He was going to start a new school the next day, and he and his friends felt they had to act tough only because they were really scared.

Classes went smoothly the first day and have every day since. But Charlie makes sure he doesn't do anything to draw attention to himself. Clothes play a very important part. He has to dress as the rest of the students do "or they'll make fun of you," he'll say. Every morning he'll also ask his mother for gum. Apparently, that's the hottest thing at the high school. Although his parents have not received any reports from school regarding grades, they have received notice of his attendance record. Charlie and many other migrant students have not been participating in physical education. The excuse they give is that they don't have proper attire or that in Texas they don't have to participate in P.E. if they don't want to. Neither reason is true. The real reason they don't care for physical education is because it means interacting with the other students.

"In the classroom you don't have to talk to the other students, but P.E. is different. You have to talk to them and be with them," one of Charlie's friends explained in Spanish. "And sometimes they make fun of us, they make fun of our English, and sometimes they don't want to pick us to be on their teams."

These barriers that Charlie and other migrant teenagers face on a day-to-day basis often cause them to want to quit school. Charlie has already made reference to wanting to drop out of school, but because of his parents' insistence he has continued going. In the years to come, the questions that will have to be closely examined are how long will Charlie try to fit in, and will he get discouraged enough to go through with his threats of quitting school?

As for the younger boys, what's going to happen to them when they start noticing that their peers think of them as "different"? Will they too run the risk of dropping out of school?

Of course, all this depends on how long Raul and Maria Elena continue migrating in search for work.

Night School

The Pasco School District offers night classes for high school students who work in the fields during the day. Night school runs for six weeks, from April 13 to June 2. Classes start at 5 p.m. and continue until 8:30 p.m. A bus picks up and drops off students at the labor camps. Dinner is served before night classes begin.

Currently, there are 1,315 students enrolled in Pasco High School. Of those, 175 are migrant students who attend day school; 56 migrant students attend night school.

"I believe the students that attend night school have it harder than those who go to regular day school," says Adan Tijerina, bilingual counselor and director of the night school in Pasco. "You can see a big change in the students when they arrive in the morning in comparison to those who arrive in the evenings. The morning students are boisterous and loud and the ones in the evenings are quieter, subdued. And that's because they've been working out in the fields all day."

There are requirements that night school students need to meet. They must be from a migrant family; they must not have an attendance problem (after three misses they are out of school); and they must maintain a 1.5 GPA or higher.

The majority of the migrant students are from Texas. "It's hard for them to integrate into the system when they are arriving at a time when school is almost over. They come here and it's already March or April and the regular students already know the routine and then these students come in and they have to start off fresh," Tijerina says.

To try to make the transition easier, migrant students are given an orientation. "I tell them that although they have close ties with their schools back home, they are now part of the Pasco School District. That from this moment on they are now 'perro chatos' " [bulldogs, the school's mascot].

Some of the Texas high school students who attend Pasco High will dress in cowboy boots and hats. Tijerina says he does not discourage that. "I'll wear my cowboy boots and jeans as well and I talk the same lingo as they do," the former Texan says.

Although migrant students are encouraged to integrate with other students, Tijerina says it is equally important that they maintain some bond with their school back home. One step toward this is allowing graduating seniors to wear their caps and gowns with the colors of their schools back home. This year there will be 35 migrant students graduating.

"The graduation procession is very pretty because the Pasco students walk in first and then the migrant students enter all dressed in different colors. Although this may seem like it's setting them apart it's not because they are graduating from Pasco High School, but to maintain their true identity they are wearing the colors of the school they have attended the most," Tijerina explains.

There is also a special bond that the Texas students share when they arrive in Pasco. "Back home they are all rivals because they attend different high schools, but here they are together," he says.

So far there has been no tension between the Pasco students and those who come here from Texas or other states. "Part of the reason is because every year there is such a large influx of Hispanic migrant students and the community is already used to them. They even anticipate their arrival," Tijerina explains.

In Walla Walla, where the number of high school migrant students is not as large as in Pasco, night school is not offered. There are 1,562 students enrolled in high school in Walla Walla and of that number about 90 are migrant students.

"It is difficult for these students when they first arrive, there is no doubt about that, so the teachers and counselors try to do whatever is possible to make that transition for the student easy," says Sergio Hernandez, bilingual coordinator at Walla Walla High School.

Both Tijerina and Hernandez say that as the people in the local communities get more and more accustomed to migrant families and they start seeing an interaction between migrants and non-migrants, then the transition that the young teenage migrant students have to make may be easier.

Is Education Enough?

So many times I've heard it said, "Education can mean the difference between years spent seasonally working the fields, and finding year-round employment and a better life."

Well, in my observation of the Martinez family and other migrant families, that statement may not necessarily be true. Raul and Maria Elena have 13 children. The 10 oldest are all high school graduates and have some form of vocational or technical training. Their three youngest children are currently attending school.

Maria Elena said she has always stressed education to her family, and each child realizes the importance of it. However, year after year, some members of the family still find themselves traveling to the Pacific Northwest in search of work in the fields. The reason: there are not enough jobs in their home towns, and the jobs they do find there are low in pay.

"We all like to study and we want our children to study as well. We believe in education, and it's very important for our children," Maria Elena says. "Do you think we like this kind of work and that we want this for our children? We don't. But when there is nothing else, what can you do?"

Friends and relatives of the Martinezes also have strong educational backgrounds. One male friend was an athletics coach in Mexico before coming to the United States. He speaks Spanish and English with great fluency. But once he arrived in the U.S., life became harder. It was difficult for him to find a similar job here, money was tighter, and acquiring his proper credentials meant having to fill out long forms and waiting weeks, even months, before his papers were in order. Today, he is looking for work in the potato harvest.

Another friend of the family who recently arrived in Boardman was a mortician in Mexico. He, too, suffered economic setbacks when he quit his job in Houston to go to South Texas to be closer to his family in Mexico. So now he, his wife, and their two infant daughters are traveling the country in search of work, which usually means farm labor.

"I just hope my kids don't do this the rest of their lives because it's got to stop, for everybody, not just my children. I don't think there should be any more migrants," Maria Elena says frequently.

The schooling that the Martinez children have received has been greatly beneficial, she says. Billy is getting a better command of English through the language program. Jimmy, who speaks English and Spanish fluently, does not need to be in the migrant program. Aside from getting a good, rounded education, Jimmy is being mainstreamed, which will be a necessity.

Neither speak of field work when asked "What do you want to be when you grow up?" Jimmy will most often say he wants to be a doctor, although he'll sometimes say a policeman or actor. Billy wants to serve in the armed forces. The only one who has not thought much about the question is Charlie.

"I guess I will [think about that] when I'm in high school," he said recently.

So according to Maria Elena, the only way today's migrant workers can get out of the fields and into steady jobs that offer good pay is by having those steady jobs available.

Maria Elena Martinez. *Jeff Horner*

Francisca Noriega of Mission, Texas, grades asparagus at a Green Giant plant in eastern Washington. *Isabel Valle*

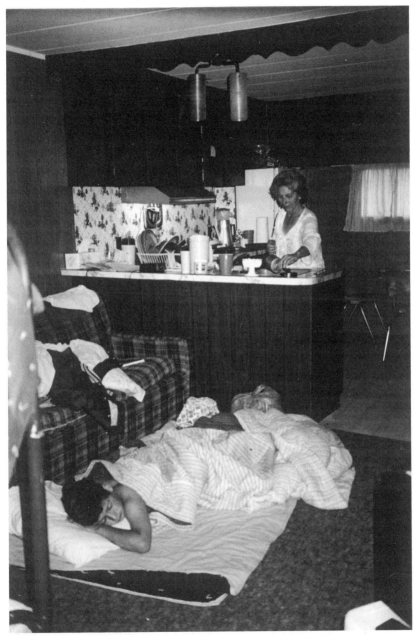

Jimmy sleeps while Maria Elena works in the kitchen. *Isabel Valle*

Ricardo Guardado, Green Giant's human resources supervisor in Pasco, Washington.
Ruben Garcia

Josten's representative Mark Stevens (l.) measuring Ricardo Barrera, of Rio Grande City, Texas, for graduation cap and gown. Roel Cardoza, of Pasco, measures Ruben Cardoza, of Weslaco, Texas, as Omar Rodriguez, of San Antonio, Texas, looks on. During the Pasco High School graduation ceremony, the seniors from migrant families wear the colors of their high schools in Texas. *Isabel Valle*

Maria Elena making a transaction at Pasco's U. S. Bank with bilingual teller Tayebeh Mostala. *Isabel Valle*

Nancy Delgado, outreach worker at La Clinica in Pasco, explains the dangers of high blood pressure and cholesterol. *U-B Photo*

Boardman teacher Christine Garcia instructs Billy Martinez (center) and other Hispanic children. *Isabel Valle*

Isabel Valle at home with the Martinezes; (l. to r.) Jimmy, Maria Elena, Isabel, Billy, and Raul. *U-B photo*

Chapter 15

Business and Community:
The Language Barrier

ONE DAY WHILE LIVING in Boardman last year, Billy came home from school looking rather gloomy. I asked what was wrong, and he told me some kids from school were making fun of him. He had been speaking in Spanish to one of his friends, and the other kids called him "dummy" because he wasn't speaking in English.

"Were they speaking to you in English?" I asked.

"Yes."

"You understood them?"

"Yes."

"Yet, they didn't understand you when you were speaking in Spanish, right?"

"Yeah."

"Well Billy, I don't think you're a dummy at all for knowing how to speak two languages. As a matter of fact, I think you're very smart," I told him. He felt a little better.

Recently I gave a speech at a local school, and before class began I was speaking in Spanish with a student from Mexico. As the rest of the students began filing in, one student looked at us and told another, "I just hate it when they do that. They're in this country now and they should speak English."

I kindly looked at him and said, "We're speaking Spanish because we feel comfortable speaking that language. Besides, this conversation is not directed toward you. And if it were, I can guarantee that every word would be in English."

The student never looked at me again, especially when I was introduced as the guest speaker. Examples of this kind are abundant, and they all point to the same thing—when people are overheard speaking Spanish, or any language other than English, the stares they get from others are of disapproval and sometimes even disgust. Being bilingual is not anything to be ashamed of. Being bilingual is a plus because that means you can communicate with twice as many people.

Granted, there are times when speaking in a foreign language can be considered rude, such as when there are three people in a room and one is being left out of the conversation. But in this community, Spanish is primarily spoken among those whose first language is Spanish.

I guess what bothers me the most is that Spanish-speaking natives are sometimes considered ignorant because they cannot get their point across in English. They're not. They have a command of the Spanish language, as others have a command of the English language.

I once learned a valuable lesson on this. While attending grade school in San Antonio, Texas, a student from Mexico enrolled in the school. Her English was limited, and like all kids, we started criticizing her. One morning our teacher called her to the front of the classroom and had her read from a book in Spanish. She did it expertly. Our teacher then called the person we considered the brightest student in the classroom to read from the same book. He struggled with every word. From that day forward, the criticism stopped. I sometimes feel this same example should be shown to adults.

In a community where more than one language is spoken, there are certain needs that must be met. In Walla Walla County, about 10 percent of the population are Hispanics, and the majority of those are Mexican natives, according to the 1990 U.S. Census. There must be bilingual personnel in places that are frequented by people who speak only Spanish; having bilingual people in businesses opens more doors and means more business. And it makes sense to have someone capable of dealing with Spanish-speaking people if that is who they associate with in their jobs.

Many times I have been asked to translate while at a grocery store or at a bank. I have even been requested to serve as a translator for social service organizations when one of their social workers had to conduct an interview with a migrant family. In the latter case, I was conducting an interview of my own at the Walla Walla Migrant Headstart Program when the social worker walked in to see if she could take one of the workers with her to help translate. They were all busy, so she asked me to help. I learned that the organization has worked with migrant families for many years. I kept repeating to myself, "So shouldn't Spanish be required from all of its employees?"

As the years go by, more and more people who speak only Spanish keep coming to Walla Walla and the surrounding area. It is in their best interest to learn the English language, but it may be profitable for local residents to learn the Spanish language as well.

Community Efforts

Some people in the Walla Walla area recognize this significant communication problem. But while some organizations have been working to combat the problem, some residents feel solutions have been slow in coming.

"There have been improvements, but we still have a long way to go," says Dan Clark, a Walla Walla attorney who represents clients who speak only Spanish.

Although it is easy for a person who speaks only Spanish to walk into a grocery store to buy food or to buy clothes at a department store, it can be difficult to purchase a car, look for housing, or seek medical care or legal help. Many companies, agencies, and organizations in the Walla Walla area do not have bilingual employees, even when they know there is a desperate need for them.

Walla Walla General Hospital and St. Mary Medical Center have a limited number of qualified, Spanish-speaking employees. Those who are bilingual usually work in admittance. The Walla Walla Police Department employs one Hispanic officer, while the College Place Police Department does not employ any bilingual people. The Walla Walla County Sheriff's Department has one Hispanic deputy, who has been with the department for almost three years.

"When it comes to dispatching we have a real problem," says a Walla Walla police department employee, who asks that her name not be used. Of the staff of 36, one person is fluent in Spanish, and five others "know a little to get by."

One way most agencies communicate with Spanish-speaking individuals is by having translators. But this has caused problems because translators often are not familiar with medical or legal terms in Spanish. Mary Lou Jenkins, employment and training coordinator at the Job Training Center, said she is often sought to serve as an interpreter. Many times she is paid for her services; other times it may be on a volunteer basis.

"I don't mind helping people where I can, but sometimes I feel a little awkward because I find that I may have to struggle to get the correct point across," Jenkins says. Also, there are times when she does not know what situation she's going to be placed in.

One morning recently she was called by the College Place Police Department to help interpret. "I have no idea what this is about or what I'm about to face," she said on the way to the police station. Upon her arrival she was told the case involved a minor complaint against a resident. She followed the police officer to a nearby home, and when the woman in the house opened the door Jenkins began the questioning. The officer stood nearby, jotting in his note pad the information Jenkins gave him. After a few minutes of questioning, Jenkins thanked the woman for her time and she and the officer left the house. The officer then thanked Jenkins for her time and drove away. "This happens all the time," Jenkins said as she got in her car.

Jenkins and other local Hispanic residents feel the community is not meeting the needs of the monolingual, Spanish-speaking population.

"First off, it's clearly obvious that people who do not speak English are treated differently around here. They are treated rudely by others in the community," Jenkins says. "I know a lot of monolingual people who will not enter certain banks and stores because of how they are treated."

Frank Herrera of Blue Mountain Translation Service agrees. "Until this town recognizes that these people are worth more than just onion pickers, then I don't think we'll see any movement toward providing for them. These people pump a lot of money into the economy. But the community has a tendency to ignore that."

Herrera and Jenkins say they are often asked by Spanish-speaking people to translate for them when they are in the hospital, or to speak with their landlords or purchase items. Clark, a bilingual attorney, said he too has been asked many times to serve as a translator in instances other than legal affairs, but he feels unqualified.

"Why? is what I always ask myself," Herrera says. "The fact that we're always asked to translate just tells me that the community is not working to fill a definite void. And, on top of that, those that serve as translators are not recognized for their expertise."

But some disagree, saying they are trying to find solutions. About a year ago, St. Mary Medical Center installed an AT&T Language Line in the emergency room. The Language Line works as a conference call. The patient or family member sits in a room with the doctor and a bilingual phone operator does all the translating.

"This has really proven beneficial because you can see the look of relief in someone's face when they hear someone speaking Spanish, and they don't have to feel frustrated because they can't get their point across," says Susan Leathers, director of Clinical Care Services at the hospital.

Marilee Town, director of public affairs at the St. Mary center, says that prior to the Language Line, patients had to come into the hospital with their own interpreters—in some cases, the interpreters being their own children.

"Granted, there were a lot of difficulties. Sometimes we couldn't get qualified translators and we found that things weren't being translated as they should have been. And there were a lot of gaps in the information that was being given and taken," Town explains.

Walla Walla General Hospital has some of its brochures written in Spanish. It also provides Spanish instructional videos on childbirth and child rearing, and also uses translators.

Both the Walla Walla and College Place police departments use translators when needed. The College Place police department utilizes a Dallas-based law enforcement television training program that teaches key Spanish phrases and words that officers may hear when stopping someone.

"Translators are great. But are these people qualified?" Jenkins asks. "Being bilingual and being a qualified translator are two different things. If you don't know legal or medical terms and you're not passing the right information, you can be getting yourself into a lot of trouble."

Hispanic residents feel the only way to erase this problem is by hiring Hispanic, bilingual employees. The police departments and the hospitals say more bilingual people are not hired because none have applied for jobs when they are available.

"My response to that is, 'Are you looking in the right place?' " Jenkins asks. "You're not going to find anyone if you don't know where to look. It's like trying to find an orange in an apple orchard."

Clark, the attorney representing Spanish-speaking clients, agrees. "How many times do companies establish bilingualism as a practical requirement? I think that extra effort by the employer has to be taken to find someone to fill these positions."

According to Jenkins, "Employers need to advertise in Hispanic magazines that circulate throughout the country. It only makes sense that if you can't find someone in the local community, then you go to the outside and find somebody."

There are two sides to the issue of monolingualism, according to Clark. "First, you have a number of people who have lived here many years and who still don't know English and haven't attempted to learn it. And on the other side, you have people who resent migrants and feel that there isn't any reason to help them. These are two different ends of the spectrum, and what has to happen is that the community has to band together to fight this problem."

One business that has made a rather large dent in the language barrier is banking.

User-Friendly Banking

In a black trunk, under lock and key, Raul and Maria Elena keep most every penny that they own. When they need money for groceries, gas, children's clothes, or for emergencies Maria Elena unlocks the trunk and pulls out a white envelope that contains almost all their money. She leafs through the bills and pulls out the amount that will be needed. Then she carefully counts what is left before putting the money back in the envelope and placing it under lock and key in the trunk.

For years the Martinez family has safeguarded its money this way. Other migrant families are known to hide their earnings in mattresses or under a loose brick or board in their homes. Up until the past couple of years there was no such thing as having a bank account. But financial institutions in communities where there are large migrant populations are making strides toward getting farm workers into their offices. For the past five years, bilingual employees with U.S. Bank have been leaving their teller windows to climb into the back of pickup trucks and head out to the fields.

"We go to the farmer's place of business, whether it be an office, a machine shed, or actually out into the field, to explain our services to the workers," says Carl Leth, U.S. Bank's Tri-Cities district vice president and manager. "One of the main points we try to get across is that by establishing a savings account the farm workers are able to make money and they don't have to carry it around."

Most migrant workers don't want bank accounts because they feel easy access to their cash would be restricted. Migrant workers also feel intimidated by banking procedures that are hard to understand, especially when everything is written in English.

"We know that communication has been a problem, so to combat that we've hired bilingual tellers, our brochures are in Spanish, and last year we even installed bilingual automatic teller machines," Leth says.

Other banks have noticed the importance of bilingualism and have been working to attract Hispanic customers, including migrant workers. Baker Boyer Bank in Walla Walla, for example, has been holding seminars with the migrant community to answer questions regarding banking transactions.

"Late last year we started developing relations with KSMX Radio [the only local Spanish language radio station] to try to find out how we can address the migrant community or to see if we could answer any questions," explains Mark Hess, marketing director at Baker Boyer Bank. "We found out that they were frustrated with the system and banking is hard to understand. So we had to make an effort to learn how to explain banking and its terminology in Spanish."

The efforts have proven beneficial. For the past few years, more migrant workers have walked through the glass doors of the bank. "We have a lot of people mainly opening savings accounts, and they are very pleased that we have a few tellers that speak Spanish so their questions can be answered," says Irma Aranda, a bilingual teller at Baker Boyer. "They go tell their family and friends that there is someone at the bank that speaks Spanish, so that brings in more customers to see us."

Other banks, including the Seafirst and First Interstate branches in Walla Walla, are printing brochures in Spanish and hiring bilingual tellers. "We recognize that this is an important market and a growing market, so for the past couple of years we have been taking steps toward addressing the Hispanic community," says Steve Truscott, vice president and manager of Seafirst Bank in Walla Walla. For employees who want to learn the language, Seafirst pays tuition to enroll in up to four quarters of Spanish classes.

But even with banking procedures explained in Spanish, some migrant workers are still skeptical about having a total stranger take care of their money.

"We know that they don't want to let go of their money, that they may not like the idea of having someone else 'hold on' to their money, and that they feel uncomfortable not having their money at arm's length," U.S. Bank's Leth says. "So we try to point out that while they are here they can have a savings account where their money will grow interest and once they leave they can take their money with them. Their account will stay dormant for a couple of months. But once they come back the next year, they will have their account here waiting for them."

Last year the Martinez family opened an account with U.S. Bank. "We did it mainly so that we could cash our checks without having to pay anything. And when we left we only kept about $5 in the account," Maria Elena explains, adding that the family still keeps most of its money locked away in the storage trunk.

Leth says the bank truly is interested in taking care of migrant workers' financial needs, which is hard to explain to the workers. "Sure, this is a business and like all businesses we want to succeed. But at the same time we want to know how we can better communicate with the migrant community."

Leth continues, "We want to know if they feel comfortable when they walk into a bank and if they know what to expect. And I think they realize that, once they see that our employees are willing to go out into the fields and talk to them on their lunch breaks. The workers see that we are making an effort to talk to them and are not just inside a bank waiting for them to come in."

One night recently, the bank in Pasco remained open late to assist the migrant community. "We know these people work seven days a week and are out in the fields when we're open – and we're closed by the time they get home and rest," Leth says. "So we decided to stay open one night until 8 p.m. We got a handful of people that had a lot of questions for us."

Since U.S. Bank began targeting the migrant community five years ago, Leth has seen an increase in business. U.S. Bank in Walla Walla is also making an attempt to draw in the migrant community. However, in Walla Walla, the numbers may be smaller because the farms employ fewer workers than the fields near Pasco.

"One of the main reasons things here may be a little more successful than in other areas is because the community as a whole provides services for the migrant workers," Leth explains. "In Pasco the schools, health clinics, grocery stores, department stores – almost everybody – realize the importance of these workers when they come into the community. The migrant workers have been coming here for years, and through the years Pasco has built such a close relationship with [the South Texas Valley], which is where most of these migrants are from."

Community Benefits

Although their true impact on the economy hasn't been measured, migrant workers surely provide a boost for some types of businesses. Grocery and retail store owners say that sales increase immediately when migrant workers arrive. Since migrant workers do not have a large income, they will spend their money on necessities such as food and clothes, and, of course, gas and parts for their vehicles.

Chuck Valdez, manager of Big Apple Food Warehouse, notes that his sales jumped by 10 percent this year once migrant workers moved into the area in early spring. Sales increased even more last year because of better crop production, which meant there were more migrant workers in the locality, he says.

Another popular place for migrants to shop is at the Safeway stores in Walla Walla and Milton-Freewater. Store managers say it is difficult to determine actual sales during the time when migrants return; however, they say there is an increase during the spring and summer months. "When seasonal workers are in the area, we do see some improvement in business," indicates John Blakely, district manager for Safeway in Yakima.

Several state agencies contacted by the *Walla Walla Union-Bulletin* had not collected statistics to indicate the economic impact that migrant farm workers have on the region. However, it's clear that once most of the crops have been harvested and the winter months are not far ahead, sales begin to wane and businesses plan for the decline.

In Milton-Freewater, the store that probably feels the most impact is 3-Amigos Bakery located at 123 E. Broadway. Although specific figures cannot be provided, owner Ramiro Zuniga says business slows down a bit when migrant workers are not in the area. 3-Amigos Bakery is popular among Hispanic migrants because of the types of products it carries. On stock are candies, herbs, teas, and soft drinks brought directly from Mexico. Most of the canned goods and non-perishables also are packaged in Mexico; therefore, labels are written in Spanish. Sweet bread, very popular among Hispanics, and Mexican and Tejano music, pinatas, zarapes, and pottery can also be found in the little corner store.

Although stores may feel a pinch in their sales during the fall and winter, business booms at the Greyhound Bus station in Walla Walla.

A ticket agent said a lot of people take advantage of specials, including one-way tickets to Texas that cost $68. Without special fares, a one-way ticket costs around $200.

Chapter 16

Migrant Women: Never-Ending Toil

These men have the women as slaves. You walk into a Hispanic migrant home and you see the woman doing every single thing in the house...and the husband is just sitting there sleeping or watching television. It really gets you angry, especially when the women can't see that they don't have to live that way.

— Nancy Delgado, outreach worker, La Clinica Migrant Health Center, Pasco

THEY BEGIN THEIR DAYS in the kitchen, and 18 hours later can still be found washing those last pots and pans before settling in for some sleep. During the day they wash and iron clothes, clean the house, bathe and look after children, serve as hostesses to visitors, and run errands. Aside from all this, many of them also spend as much as 10 hours a day working in the fields under the hot, glaring sun. The role of Hispanic females in the migrant community is considered by some non-migrant men and women as a job that's twice as hard as that of the males.

"I know a lot of women who are up at the crack of dawn, and it is non-stop until they go to sleep at night," says Duane Page, field representative with Green Giant. "I've asked their husbands why they don't help them a bit around the house, and they all say, 'Because it's their job.' What has always bothered me is that the women are doing the exact same job as the men. They are out there in the fields working side-by-side, right along with their husbands."

Women who labor in the agricultural plots often earn the same amount as their husbands, and men and women are considered equals while in the fields. A typical day for a migrant woman may go as follows—Wake up at 3 a.m. to prepare breakfast and lunch for the family. This usually includes making a stack of fresh flour tortillas. An hour later she wakes up the rest of the family. If she has children, she takes them to a day care center, or to a neighbor or relative who will care for them during the day. If the children are school age, a neighbor usually will make sure they get to school on time. At about 4:30 a.m., she climbs into the truck or car with the rest of the workers in her family and proceeds to the fields. It's usually 1 or 2 p.m. when the field work has been completed, and they all return home. She immediately heads for the kitchen, where she warms up the lunch she cooked in those early morning hours. After lunch, the house chores begin. There are dishes to be washed, laundry, sweeping, dusting, mopping, and scrubbing to be done, and clothes to fold and put away. Some days she must go grocery shopping, buy clothes for members of the family, visit the bank, or go to the post office. All this must be completed by 4 p.m., when the children return home from school or are picked up from the day care center. Then it's back to the kitchen, where another stack of fresh flour tortillas is made. Dinner is cooked and served. After all have eaten, she washes dishes again. In the evening, she must bathe the children, iron their clothes for the next day, and help them with homework. Other workers living nearby may drop by for a visit, and she must serve as their hostess. A fresh pot of coffee must be brewed. Snacking usually goes on until 9 p.m., so the sink is stacked with dishes once again. Before she lies down to rest, the babies must be put to sleep, bottles have to be prepared, and the kitchen has to be cleaned one last time. She tries to get to sleep before 10 p.m., because in five hours it all starts again.

A typical day for a man goes as follows—At 4 a.m. he wakes up, eats, and goes to the fields, working until 1 or 2 p.m. Then he returns home, takes a shower, changes clothes, and eats lunch. It is then time for a short nap. At about 3 or 4 p.m. he wakes up, goes outside to wash his truck or car, and makes sure it's in good working condition. After dinner, he may settle in to watch television, finish working on his vehicle, or visit neighbors. By 9 p.m. he is already in bed.

Women do not think it is unusual for themselves to take on the full responsibility of caring for the household and children. When they gather together, there is never any complaining; instead they speak about it as if it is their duty.

"We all began cooking and cleaning and looking after the men in the house at a very early age, about 10 or so. And our mothers did it and their mothers did it, so that's how we are," Fedencia Barrera, 46, says in Spanish. "And that's the way I raised my daughter, and that's how I expect my daughters-in-law to be."

Maria Elena is also very proud that her three married daughters and four daughters-in-law are all working women and caretakers of the home and family.

" 'Son amas de casa' [they're homemakers], and that's the way Raul wanted them raised. And they all take care of their husbands real well," Maria Elena says proudly. Most of her daughters and daughters-in-law work full time, then go home in the evenings to cook, clean, wash, and look after their children.

"They would never think of their husbands helping them out in the kitchen or around the house. And if Raul ever found out that they [the men] were doing the work that their wives should be doing, he would get very angry," Maria Elena explains.

Within the Hispanic migrant community, women learn at an early age that housework is their responsibility alone, and that men do not lift a finger to help. The thought of them doing so is considered "unmanly."

But sometimes the situation may become abusive. Nurses and social workers who deal with women in the migrant community say they often see cases where women are treated like slaves. Registered nurse Margaret Caicedo of Walla Walla's Family Medical Center has worked with cases where young girls are kept out of school or even brought from Mexico to take care of their home and family.

"I know of three families [in Walla Walla and in Milton-Freewater] where girls are taken out of school to serve as housekeepers and child care providers. In one family, a 14-year-old niece was brought over here from Mexico to purposely take care of the family of eight and the house," Caicedo says.

Caicedo, who also works with the Maternal Support Service program offered by the center, has seen many cases of emotional and physical abuse. "I know this is found in all economic levels, but I think that Hispanic women in the migrant community have it the worst," she points out. "Men will convince their wives that they have no other option but to stay in the situation that they are in, and many times the women feel they have nowhere to go. The woman has a lot of kids, she has no papers, and she has very limited English skills, so she feels she can't get out," Caicedo explains. "Also, the husbands will get themselves legalized – but they won't do that for their wives."

Nancy Delgado (outreach worker at La Clinica Migrant Health Center in Pasco) agrees that the man is the dominant figure in the household and that women generally have no say in the relationship:

"These men have the women as slaves. You walk into a Hispanic migrant home and you see the woman doing every single thing in the house. . . And the husband is just sitting there sleeping or watching television," Delgado says. "It really gets you angry, especially when the women can't see that they don't have to live that way."

Caicedo feels a major part of the problem is the macho image portrayed by the Hispanic male. "The man's self-esteem is so low here because he can't get a good job, he's struggling financially, he can't even get his point across at a grocery store because of his English skills, so he's really under a lot of stress. That does not excuse him, but I feel that is one of the reasons he becomes so abusive."

Some contend that it is not only the machismo image, but the fact that the men and women have been brought up this way.

"A lot of men grew up seeing their fathers and grandfathers being the dominant ones in the family, and the women themselves saw that as children. So they grow up seeing this as part of the relationship," points out Jackie Morales, case manager at the family medical center. "Another major factor is that women feel intimidated because their own family members are not supportive," Morales adds. "Young women have their mothers telling them, 'He's your husband now, and you have to do what he says and you have to put up with everything.' "

Social workers believe that until today's women decide to no longer follow the traditional Hispanic female role, women are going to continue taking on all the responsibilities that are imposed on them by Hispanic males.

An Outsider's View

Submissive. Dutiful. Obedient. Restricted. Those were the words that came to mind when I first moved into the migrant community almost a year ago. I was appalled at how women serve and wait on men from head to toe without any questions asked.

When I first moved in with the Martinez family, I became one of two females in a house with four males. Raul immediately expected me to take on the role that he expects from all women. That meant I had to wake up before dawn to help his wife in the kitchen. During the day, I had to wash, cook, and clean, and tend to the children. I was not to talk back to any of the men, even when I disagreed with them, and I was not to air my opinion. At first I did what was expected until I saw that women were treated distinctly different from men.

"Women shouldn't go to school. What for? As long as they know how to cook and be housewives, that's what's important so that they can get married," Raul once told me. "And a woman works because she wants to. She should stay at home to take care of her children, her house, and her husband."

We always got into heated arguments when I spoke about women going on to college, getting a good education, and having a career. "Back home, women who do that do not have a very good reputation," Maria Elena would say.

It was hard for me to accept this type of lifestyle because of my upbringing. I come from a family with three daughters, and education was extremely important to our parents. The need for a college education was embedded in us at a very early age. I remember my father repeating to us, "You have to get a good education and get into a good career so you can stand on your own two feet."

If that meant leaving our homes and traveling thousands of miles, our parents were always there to support and encourage us. At home, household responsibilities were equally shared by my parents. And in the same respect, my mother often helped my father with the plumbing and electrical work.

My family is not an exception. There are many Hispanic families that have the same beliefs. But the Hispanic migrant families I associated with for one year held views distinctly different from mine.

In Hispanic migrant households, the men in the family are not expected to lift one finger to help around the house. I once asked 11-year-old Jimmy to fold the blankets he slept on the night before. "No. That's a woman's job," he responded. I also asked Billy, 7, to pick up his plate after he finished eating and place it in the kitchen sink. I got the same response. Maria Elena overheard the conversations. She decided to fold the blankets and pick up the plate herself. But before she did, I gently got ahold of the boys, took them into the bedroom and gave them a little lecture. They ended up doing the chores themselves. Raul never verbally complained when I gave the boys household chores to do, but I often got cold stares from him.

Many nights, Maria Elena would already be asleep when either her husband or one of her sons would get her out of bed to iron a shirt for them for the next day. She would do it without complaining. Sometimes, in the middle of her dinner, Raul or one of her sons would be showering and would call out for her to bring a towel or clean clothes. She would stop eating and take them what they wanted. She did this without complaining.

At what I considered an extreme, Maria Elena once even stopped eating lunch to go put socks on her husband because he kept screaming from his bed that he was cold and his feet were bare. Again, she did this without complaining.

"That's the way we are. That's the way we have been brought up. The women do everything in the house," she said.

"To do everything in the house is one thing, but to put socks on your husband's feet because he doesn't want to do it himself?" I practically screamed at the top of my lungs!

She just looked at me and shrugged her shoulders.

While we were spending the winter in Texas, Maria Elena would talk about not returning north this year and instead staying at home with her children and looking after her ailing mother. Then she would erase the thought from her mind saying, "No. Raul would die without me out there. Who would cook for him and take care of him?"

The Hispanic migrant women I have come to know are also not allowed to leave the home while their husbands are at work. If Maria Elena or any of the women in the labor camp ever needed to run an errand, it had to be done after their husbands were at work and before they came home—and without their husbands knowing about it. If they did go on an errand when their husbands were at home, many husbands would time how long it would take for them to finish the errand.

Many husbands were also reluctant to let their wives spend time with me because, aside from my bosses at the newspaper, I had no one keeping tabs on me. I guess they were afraid where I would take them or what I would tell them. I got used to all the dirty looks I often got from the husbands.

In Texas, things were even worse. In the hometowns where these people live the mentality is, "A woman's place is in the kitchen." And it's taken literally. During family gatherings, the men would be outside while all the women were in the kitchen. The two groups never mixed.

I was once invited to a political gathering at a candidate's home. As I walked in, I saw all the men sitting in the living room discussing local politics, something I was very interested in. After I was introduced to all the men in attendance, I was told by the candidate, "The women are in the kitchen. I think that's where you probably want to be."

I looked at him and said, "Actually, I think I'd find your discussion much more interesting than the recipes that are being exchanged in the kitchen. So if you don't mind I'd rather stay here." After a few minutes of disapproving stares and the apparent uneasiness that was shown by the men, I decided to leave the room and go into the kitchen.

My reputation in the tiny towns that line the South Texas border was that of someone who always spoke her mind and did not follow the traditional Hispanic female role. Maria Elena eventually learned to accept the kind of lifestyle that my mother and father ingrained in me: women are individuals and can be independent, career-minded people. Raul, however, still has problems with that.

Chapter 17

Conclusion: Slow Progress

IN THE EARLY 1960s when journalist Edward R. Murrow presented the documentary "Harvest of Shame" on television, the bleak reality of migrant life was exposed. The television audience saw farm workers piled into trucks, traveling thousands of miles in search of work; they saw migrant families living in scantily furnished, two-room shacks, often without indoor plumbing; and they were told about the hardships migrant children endured and how they made up one of the most underrepresented groups in education.

Thirty years later, after spending a year residing in the migrant community, I saw little change between the film and the life that farm workers follow today. True, progress has been made by those who fight for the plight of the migrant worker, but they say these improvements are merely dents in the system, and that much more still needs to be done.

Education

Issues involving migrant children have remained a major concern, with a focus on education. Because of this attention, many federal- and state-funded programs have been developed to assist these children. The first development in this regard occurred in 1960, when federal dollars were funnelled to states with large numbers of migrant workers. The money paid for modular classrooms that were turned into day care centers for migrant children.

Today, there are a number of educational programs available for children. The Migrant Head Start Program serves bilingual and bicultural children from infancy through age five, monitoring their physical, dental, and mental health needs. The Chapter 1 Migrant Education Program helps students make a smooth transition from one school to another, offers individualized instruction and bilingual classes, and provides a nationwide computerized network where records of students aged 3 to 10 are maintained and forwarded to the various schools they attend. The National Migrant Student Records Transfer System also keeps the child's health and family data.

Other educational plans include the Seasonal Farm Worker Child Care Program, Migrant Farm Worker AIDS Education and Prevention Program, and the Hispanic Farm Workers Child Abuse Prevention Project. English as a Second Language is also available to migrant workers, as well as to people from other cultures.

In the 1970s, federal assistance was extended to the college level with the College Assistance Migrant Program (CAMP), offering freshman-year assistance. Several universities now participate in CAMP in Oregon, Idaho, Texas, California, and Colorado. CAMP is funded by the U.S. Department of Education, the various states, and the participating universities.

Child Labor

While some strides have been made toward improving the life of farm workers and their children, many problems they faced decades ago are still common today. The agricultural child labor regulations instituted in Washington in July 1990 are different than regulations governing children in non-farming employment. Youths under the age of 16 are limited to a maximum of 18 hours of work during school weeks, while those employed in agricultural jobs may work as many as 21 hours a week. Children employed in non-agricultural jobs may work only five days a week, while those working in the fields may work six days a week. Although the rules are set up to protect children, some advocates say laws should specifically prohibit kids from working before school.

Health

Health problems still plague migrant workers, who suffer from Third World afflictions—parasitic diseases, salmonella, polio, and yellow fever—as well as diabetes, cardiovascular diseases, and asthma. These illnesses are the result of, among other things, poor nutrition, lack of resources, accidents, overcrowding, and poor sanitation. The life expectancy of a migrant worker is 48 years.

Medical providers believe a networking system should be developed within the medical community, allowing for the health records of migrants to be transferred electronically from one clinic to another, depending on where the families relocate. Right now, migrant families have to take on the responsibility of returning to clinics and obtaining their test results and other medical files. Then they must carry these medical records everywhere they go.

Housing

One of the biggest problems migrants still face is inadequate housing. Many today live under the same conditions faced by migrants in the 1950s. Some reside in overcrowded rental units; others dwell under bridges, in makeshift shelters constructed of cardboard; others make their home in one-room shacks, or old army barracks that have been converted into studio apartments. Many of these places are filled with roaches, rats, and other rodents, have one hole in the ground for cooking, and another hole in the ground for a toilet.

Outlook

Advocates of migrant rights say much still needs to be done to improve the quality of life for field workers, but, before that can be accomplished, the mentality of the general American population needs to change. "We can go back and see where improvements have been made with individual families or people, but as a whole nothing within the migrant community has changed," said Roberta Ryder, executive director of the National Migrant Resource Program.

She notes that the same problems migrant workers faced 30 years ago are still being faced by the migrant workers of today: "The problems are the same, only the faces changed." Ryder believes that increased public awareness must develop before extensive improvement can occur.

Parting

Saturday, June 20, 11 a.m. The car turns onto a dirt road that leads away from the Pasco labor camp. In the trunk are my suitcases and other personal items I have been storing at the Martinez trailer for the past month. I moved away a month ago so the separation between myself and the family would be gradual. Even though I no longer live with the Martinezes, I have visited at least twice a week. Keeping some of my belongings there helped maintain a sense of closeness between us.

I return this morning to pick up my things, since the family will soon pack their belongings and move. The asparagus season has ended, and they don't know where they're going. Work is scarce throughout this area, and housing is even harder to find.

I am with a friend who is behind the steering wheel. In the car, driving away from the camp, there is no talking. No music. Just silence. The car windows are rolled down and the hot air hits our faces. We see the camp getting smaller and smaller in the rearview mirror. There is a lump in my throat. I have a feeling of emptiness inside. I find myself blinking to fight back tears. I turn to my friend. . .tears roll down her cheeks. "They will always see you as a daughter," she tells me.

For the next 45 minutes on the road back to Walla Walla, and throughout the rest of the day, I reflect on the past year.

I got off the plane in Walla Walla on April 22, 1991, with two suitcases in my hands. I knew no one. I knew nothing about the community. I had never been to the northwest part of the United States before. Fourteen months later, I hardly have enough room in my car to fit half the things I've accumulated. I've made a lot of friends in Walla Walla and surrounding areas, and I've traveled throughout the Northwest.

But most importantly, I met a family that will always have a special place in my heart. The Martinezes—Raul, Maria Elena, Charlie, Jimmy, and Billy—whom I'll always see as my adopted parents and younger brothers. There are 13 children in the family, but the three boys were the ones I got close to, since they are the ones who still travel with their parents.

This is not to say it was an easy year, because it wasn't. This was the hardest assignment I've agreed to in my eight years as a newspaper reporter. It's not easy bringing together total strangers under one roof and having them live together for one year. Before I moved in with the family, the only thing I knew about them was their names, where they were from, and what they did for a living. They knew as little about me. Before I moved in with them, I was used to being on my own. Living with the Martinezes, I now had "parents" who expected me to do as they said—and I had three younger brothers who sometimes drove me nuts.

I remember the first time I met Maria Elena in early June 1991. She was doing laundry in the Pasco labor camp. I considered her to be spunky, cheerful, and enthusiastic. A few days later I met her husband, Raul. He was equally as pleasant and always had a smile on his face. As the year went by Maria Elena and I became good friends, but we did have our disagreements. Raul and I also had numerous heated arguments, but Maria Elena was always there to calm tempers. She was very tactful when it came to showing her disapproval of things I said or did. Raul was more direct.

As for the boys. . .

Charlie, 16, was the hardest to get to know, but now we're good friends. It took about two months after I moved in before he even acknowledged my presence. Before then he refused to speak with me, look at me, or even be in the same room with me. But after a lot of insisting on my part, he opened up. Now, he and I joke around when we're together. His birthday was earlier this month. For a present he wants me to give him my car. . .or buy him a new one.

Jimmy, 11, was the warmest, and we became friends immediately. He always accompanied me places – the grocery store, the post office, the movies, the county fair. Throughout the year, he always told me to visit the family after this project is completed. I will.

Billy, 8, became my little brother from the first moment I walked in the door. The first night we sat together and read from one of his school books. Many times I was in my bedroom writing or reading, and he would quietly walk in with all his toys and start playing by himself. He used to walk around the house looking for things to give me. I will always treasure a small rubber ball and key chain he presented to me.

But things were not always rosy. I detested losing my privacy and my own identity. Members of the family never knocked when they walked into my bedroom, and I often caught them looking through my things. They took an interest in my well-being, but sometimes it became suffocating. I couldn't make a single move without everybody knowing where I was every minute of the day.

While we lived in Texas during the winter, life became even harder. There, I was in their territory. While we were traveling, everyone was away from home; so we all relied on one another for emotional support. In Texas they were at home, and that's when I really felt like an intruder, an outsider.

The entire Martinez family was very nice to me: all the sons and daughters, in-laws, nieces and nephews, grandmother, cousins, aunts and uncles. But I never felt at home. Yet I have maintained contact with them since we left Texas three months ago, and I probably always will.

To me the most difficult part of the project was the constant relocating. It was emotionally hard for me to live somewhere, get close to someone, then say goodbye.

But I learned valuable lessons from migrant workers. I learned they feel safe and comfortable anyplace they live, as long as they have their loved ones with them. I even surprised myself to learn that in every new place we moved into, I only needed to hang a few pictures of my real family to make that room feel like home. I didn't care if there wasn't any furniture and I had to sleep on the floor.

Most importantly, I learned that migrant workers are proud people. I especially see that in Raul. He takes great pride that he is still able to do hard, manual labor at the age of 62. Even the women are proud that they can do the same work as a man, then come home and take care of the house and family. In my eyes, the women I got to know are the backbone of the family and the ones who keep everyone together. I truly believe that if it weren't for the women, some of these families would fall apart.

On July 1, 1991, I walked into the Martinez household not knowing a thing about them. As I drive away from the labor camp on this hot Saturday morning almost a year later, I feel like their daughter leaving home for the first time. I never thought I would admit this, but I'm going to miss them. I remember many times during the year when I kept telling myself, "I can't wait until this is over!"

But now that my assignment has come to an end, telling them goodbye was a lot harder than I thought. I'm going to miss the constant bickering that went on between everyone in the house, as well as all the brother-sister arguments we had, as goes on in most families. I'm going to miss the fussing Maria Elena did over me as my real mother does when I was sick, or when I came home after being gone for a weekend. And I will miss Raul—whom I will always refer to as "Senor Martinez" out of respect—and the way he always made sure my car was in good working condition, the way my real father does.

Chapter 18

Epilogue

By Carrie Hartman
Business/Agriculture Reporter, *Walla Walla Union-Bulletin*

IN A SMALL, crumbling trailer ensconced on the fringes of the farm labor camp, the quiet hardships of the Martinez family's nomadic life are found.

Maria Elena keeps her collectibles – perfume bottle figurines – in boxes to prepare for immediate departure. Even the youngest child, Billy, 8, is accustomed to the frequent goodbyes, she said in a recent interview. Maria Elena began to reflect on the effects of one year of newspaper coverage through the "Fields of Toil: A Migrant Family's Journey" series.

"We've had our lives in boxes for so long it's natural for us," she says. "But we still hate to see our children have to do this."

For over 35 years, the Martinez family has brought a small clan of its 13 children to work in the fields, enduring struggles as migrant workers that often went undocumented and unnoticed. But for the past year – filled with packing, unpacking, and the endless search for work in the Pacific Northwest's agricultural towns – they found themselves on the living room coffee tables of middle American families because of the "Fields of Toil" articles.

Now, 4,500 miles and one year later, a slice of the Martinez family story is told. Reporter Isabel Valle, who faced just as much of a personal challenge as a professional one, says that life on the road took its toll. "The worst part of the project was not knowing from one day to the next where we were going," she says. "It was a very difficult year."

Other challenges existed in completely altering Valle's lifestyle. "I can't help but think that in many ways, the project was harder on me than it was for the Martinezes," she points out. "I had to change my lifestyle completely. I lost a lot of myself and my independence."

Still, after assessing the year, Valle feels the project did what it set out to do. "I think more people are aware," she feels. "If the project opened one person's eyes to be more sympathetic to the migrants, then it served its purpose."

It is this exposure of migrant life to the general public, Maria Elena says, that makes the hardships a little easier to bear. And increased attention, she notes, may be the crux of change for migrants.

"We feel more people know about migrants now, and that is good," she exclaims. "Maybe they can help us."

There wasn't much debate between Raul and his family on whether to welcome another person—this time a newspaper reporter—into their tiny quarters, says Maria Elena. Valle was viewed as a welcome addition to the Martinez "familia." "We want other people to know what our lives are like," Maria Elena explains in Spanish. "Even though we are poor, we wanted Isabel here. We are not ashamed of what we do."

But the decision to welcome the attention didn't go uncriticized by fellow migrant workers, Maria Elena adds. Raul agrees, simply nodding on his way out of the room.

"A lot of people said no before us," she says. "And when we said yes, the migrant community did not like it at first."

Valle felt the tension and reluctance of the other migrant workers. "People were hesitant to walk into the house and talk freely with the family," she says.

Living with a newspaper reporter was sometimes difficult, Maria Elena explains, but only because of reactions by their peers to Valle's questions and sometimes controversial stories surrounding gender roles, health care, and working conditions.

"Isabel told of our problems with unfair wages and the hard work we do without making us tell her. She found out for herself."

Still, the Martinez family fears repercussions from farm labor camp managers because of the "Fields of Toil" series. "We are afraid we won't be allowed back to work in Pasco anymore," Maria Elena says. "I don't want to be blamed for the problems of migrant workers or the working conditions here. I am afraid for my family because this is a place we're used to coming."

But Valle's presence gave migrant families—especially the Martinezes—a "voz," or voice. "I think people are more aware of what everyday life is like for us," Maria Elena points out. "The more people who are aware, the better."

Family members attributed the newspaper coverage for improving working conditions within the farm labor camps and encouraging workers to seek higher wages. During asparagus harvest, migrant workers took their complaints of low wages to the growers, Maria Elena says, and publicized allegations of unfair wage practices in the local media.

Billy, the youngest of the Martinez clan, says he wants a better life for his family and his brothers, Jimmy and Charlie. Spending time with Isabel may have helped the family. "It would be neat to be able to stay in Texas," he says.

Spending the past year in the media's eye brought the issues of migrant workers to the forefront for discussion. But Maria Elena feels the project only sets the groundwork. "Not much has changed since I was a migrant as a child. God knows what is in the future for our people unless we continue to do something. A lot of people are tired. They are just tired."

Departing from the "Fields of Toil" project will be difficult, especially for Billy, his mother says. Valle was "adopted" by the Martinezes, who saw her as a daughter first. Considering her a journalist documenting their lives was secondary. "Our year with Isabel allowed us and other migrants to get attention that was a long time in coming. But I will miss her laughter the most."

The migrant worker's "voz"—unearthed in "Fields of Toil" during the last year—may be softer now that the project is over, Maria Elena says, but the hardships are still there.

That much was evident as Valle departed and the Martinez family, facing a lack of jobs in the fields and no housing in Boardman, made plans to return to LaGrulla. The Martinez family had been expecting to move to Boardman. But the potato farm that has traditionally hired them for hoeing and harvesting did not plant this year, Valle says. Consequently, the Martinezes decided to return to their hometown to find work. They left June 29.

"They usually wait until October or November before they head back to LaGrulla," Valle says. "But there is absolutely no work."

Index